INDIAN LABOR
IN THE SPANISH INDIES

Was There Another Solution?

PROBLEMS IN LATIN AMERICAN CIVILIZATION

UNDER THE EDITORIAL DIRECTION OF
EDWIN LIEUWEN, UNIVERSITY OF NEW MEXICO

INDIAN LABOR IN THE SPANISH INDIES — Was There Another Solution? — *Edited by John Francis Bannon, S.J., Saint Louis University*

THE BOURBON REFORMERS AND SPANISH CIVILIZATION — Builders or Destroyers? — *Edited by Troy S. Floyd, University of New Mexico*

Other volumes in preparation

PROBLEMS IN LATIN AMERICAN CIVILIZATION

INDIAN LABOR
IN THE SPANISH INDIES

Was There Another Solution?

EDITED WITH AN INTRODUCTION BY

John Francis Bannon, S.J. SAINT LOUIS UNIVERSITY

D. C. HEATH AND COMPANY · BOSTON

Library of Congress Catalog Card Number 66-18102

Copyright © 1966 by D. C. Heath and Company

BOSTON   ENGLEWOOD   CHICAGO   DALLAS   SAN FRANCISCO   ATLANTA

PRINTED IN THE UNITED STATES OF AMERICA
PRINTED JUNE 1966

Table of Contents

Introduction

THE story of a conquest and its sequel is much like a picture done in two halves, a diptych. One half is painted in brilliant colors, is attractive, inspiring; the other half is dark, drab, and somber. From the conqueror's point of view all is bright, thrilling, satisfying; the other side is what the less fortunate conquered sees and knows.

The lot of the conquered has never been enviable. Conquerors, even when they have avoided the excesses of brutality and sadism, have been much the same through the ages, rough and insensitive to another's pain and anguish and humiliation. Philip of Macedon and the Greeks, Julius Caesar and the Gauls, the medieval Germans and the Slavs, the Belgians and the Congolese — examples could be multiplied throughout the whole course of the human story.

The Spaniards and the Portuguese came upon the lands soon to be labeled the Americas, found folk already in possession, outmaneuvered and overpowered these Americans, and established themselves as lords of this new world. The Indians were quickly cast in the role of the conquered and subjected to all the exactions and liabilities, repressions and oppressions imposed by a conquering band.

The Spaniards had come from a society in which the gentlemen, the upper class, did not work, at least not with their hands or at menial tasks. No matter how lowly their status in the homeland, the Spaniards arriving in the New World found, to their delight, other men beneath them, men to whom they did not have to answer, men to whom they did not have to look up. It was a new and exhilarating experience for the majority of the conquistadores, few of whom had come from the upper levels of Spanish society. They saw nothing wrong about putting their new subjects to work at any task which was considered too hard or too demeaning for *un hidalgo,* whose mentality, prerogatives, and station they adopted as soon as they stepped ashore. Thus, labor became the Indians' lot. Under what circumstances and according to what patterns, time and experimentation — and ultimately royal authority — were to determine.

Even before Columbus came back to Española, on his second voyage in 1493, the problem of relationships between the Spaniards and the Indians had become a very real one. The settlers who had been left behind failed to solve it to their satisfaction — there were no survivors when the Admiral touched at La Navidad. In the next years the newcomers, with the Admiral's permission, introduced the outright enslavement of the Indians as their means of survival. Queen Isabella quickly countermanded this and formally declared the Indians her free subjects, allowing, however, that they might be encouraged to work for wages, but forbidding that they should be forced to do so — she was, after all, sending Spanish laborers to Castile's new lands who should supply the labor needs of the colony. This proved no solution at all, as her Governor Ovando was quick to see. The Indians were no more inclined to work than were the arriving Spaniards. The sixteenth century was not more than a few years old when the first of the new solutions were introduced in Española. Island practices had crystalized into firm institutions by the time the conquistadores went forth to the mainland. And grave abuses were already drawing the scathing condemnations of the friars, who from the first made themselves the champions of the rights of the Indians, their rights as men and as free vassals of the Crown.

Quickly three interest groups emerged, each with a stake in the ultimate solution: the Indians, whose position is obvious; the Crown, which wanted and needed the tribute from its newly won subject and yet was troubled in its Christian conscience; and the colonists, who worried little about the morality of the solution, provided it gave them the labor to build a society they could dominate and enjoy.

Thus, the problem of interracial relations became very complicated. The conquistador's solution has evoked many opinions, contemporary and modern, favorable and unfavorable. Some of these are gathered together in this volume as a basis for study and discussion.

The first selection in this collection is from Robert S. Chamberlain. He studies pre-conquest labor and tribute patterns among the Mayas, showing that the Spaniards were not really introducing completely new or unknown practices into the Indian civilizations. This fact does not necessarily exculpate the conquistadores, but it does to a degree lessen the blame which is laid upon them. Among the Mayas and the Aztecs, the Incas and the Chibchas, and a few other groups, the Spanish work-tribute regime meant little more than a change of masters for the "common man" in those American empires.

Lesley Byrd Simpson, whose research lecture, "Spanish Utopia," has been chosen as the second piece, has been for the past several decades the foremost Anglo-American student of the labor institutions of the Spaniards, especially in their colonial viceroyalty of New Spain (comprising all their provinces north of the Isthmus). This selection is a summary of his study and gives something of an overall picture of the problem and its solutions throughout the colonial centuries. Though often highly critical of the Spaniards, Simpson feels that the Spanish practice did have many redeeming features. In this he is quite typical of the many modern observers and commentators.

The next piece is the full text of the Laws of Burgos (1512), with the Amendments of the following year. Not only is this an early statement of the Crown position, but it also acquaints the student with one of the official documents of the period. Since few things make duller reading than quotations, long or short, from laws and administrative directives, these Laws of Burgos will be the only such selection in-

cluded. As will be noted presently, acquaintance with the New Laws of 1542 can be acquired in a less painful manner. Further, no selection will be drawn from the famous code of the Indies of 1681, *Recopilación de leyes de los reynos de las Indias*, for this and for another reason. The code can be a useful source, but it must be handled, as Clarence H. Haring, a contemporary scholar, warns, "with caution." The *Recopilación* so very frequently tells what should have been, rather than what actually was.

After initiating the reader to the Laws of Burgos, this collection samples the writings of the celebrated Bartolomé de Las Casas, the fiery, highly critical, prolific "Protector of the Indians." The matter of choice from his voluminous writings was not simple. The two selections, however, one from the *Brevísima Relación* and the second from the so-called *Octavo Remedio,* are quite indicative of the man and his position. From first to last his was the loudest voice raised in condemnation of the conquistadores and their treatment of the Indians.

Las Casas did not go unchallenged in his own or in a later day. Writing in the early seventeenth century, León Pinelo, one of the great Spanish jurists of the day, devoted an entire *libro* of his *Tratado de confirmaciones* to a refutation of many of the opinions of the Dominican. A sampling from León Pinelo is the fifth piece reproduced. A somewhat similar selection might have been taken from another seventeenth-century jurist, Juan de Solórzano Pereira, who likewise defended Crown practice; an interested student would find his *Política indiana* most enlightening.

Motolinía was a Franciscan contemporary of Las Casas. One of the Franciscan group which came to New Spain in 1524 whose members are known as "Los Doce Apóstoles," Fray Toribio is often labeled as one of the most severe contemporary critics of Las Casas. At times he was severe, especially in his *Carta al Emperador Carlos V* (1555), because he was offended by the exaggerations of the Dominican. In his own fashion, however, he was as much a champion of the Indians as was Las Casas. Even though he did not feel that Las Casas should have treated the Spaniards so harshly, he was basically no more ready to pass over their abuses. This is evident in the selection reproduced from his *Historia de los indios de la Nueva España*.

In 1542 the Crown published the famous New Laws, intended to abolish the *encomiendas* which had been given to the colonists and which were principally under the fire of the contemporary critics headed by Las Casas. This new legislation met a storm of opposition throughout the Indies and ultimately had to be withdrawn or, at the very least, seriously modified. To acquaint the student with these laws, their background and the sequel, two pieces from modern historians have been chosen, the first by Lesley Simpson and the second by Lewis Hanke, another whose extensive researches have made him an authority on this question of Indian labor. The two men are not really opponents, but they provide somewhat different views of the same segment of the Spanish colonial story.

Though the New Laws did not abolish the *encomiendas,* they did set the stage for greater recourse to another way to obtain the labor and personal services of the Indians, the *repartimiento,* or the *mita,* as it was designated in certain areas of the Indies. This practice of forced labor was on the agenda of the Third Provincial Council of Mexico (1585), a meeting of the ranking ecclesiastics of New Spain. The Franciscans presented a scathing condemnation of the practice in their Memorial to the Council fathers. An overview of this Memorial is taken from the study of Richard Stafford Poole, who is engaged in extensive research on this Third and other Mexican Provincial Councils during the colonial centuries.

The *repartimiento* and the *mita* were continued, but time brought other labor practices. A short study by Silvio Zavala, the brilliant Mexican historian, highlights these later developments. This is one of three lectures on the *encomienda* and its

sequels into which Zavala has compressed his extensive study of the Indian labor systems — these and other enlightening studies are gathered in his *New Viewpoints on the Spanish Colonization of America*. His *Encomienda indiana* is one of the classics in the field.

The final piece is one which might well inspire like studies in the future. Charles Gibson has really given us a "case study." He takes the Aztecs as his subjects and shows the labor practices in action. This would seem to be an excellent and practical way of concluding this present study.

As the reader approaches an analysis and evaluation of these selections and a possible answer to the question "Was There Another Solution?" he should be on his guard lest unconscious traces of the Black Legend (*"la layenda negra"*) influence his judgment. This propaganda of the sixteenth and later centuries colored non-Iberian judgments of Spain and the Spaniards. It is not easy to forget these traditional views which take it for granted, in an *a priori* sort of way, that the Spaniard in the Americas was cruel, greedy, stupid, bungling, fanatical, sadistic, hypocritical, and a dozen more highly uncomplimentary things. At the same time, there is no call to change the legend from black to purest white. A sense of fairness, born of an objective evaluation of the evidence, can reduce the absoluteness of the black to one of the shades along the "gray scale." The Spaniards were not complete devils; neither by the same token were they saints whom the Church has not gotten around to canonizing. Historical truth in this area, like virtue, is to be found in the middle ground. But just what and where is this middle ground?

Forced labor of the Indians was a policy which often meant practical enslavement. Today no one would advocate the practices of the conquistadores as either the most ideal or the most desirable solution of their problem. But could there have been another solution? Was the actual solution as Christian as the Crown and the jurists seemed to assert? Was it as iniquitous and immoral as Las Casas described it? Was it as absolutely necessary as the colonists claimed? To none of these questions is one able to give an unqualified yes or a categoric no.

In the mind of the Crown the solution was really meant to be a temporary one. The Indians would be put under the Spaniards that they might be better and more effectively Christianized; also they were to be forced to work until they had been conditioned to form the basis for a free labor pool. Then, it was hoped, they would work by their own choice, and for wages, at those tasks necessary for the common good of the state, society, and private enterprise.

As Zavala shows, there was indeed an evolution in the labor system toward a wage economy. But it never became sufficiently general or widely accepted. To the end, the Indian was victimized, with a measure of tacit royal approval. Was the Crown in fact too hungry for its tribute, too anxious to build an economic society in the Indies which could support and bolster a tottering economy at home?

If this was the case, could Spain have maintained her empire overseas and kept the Spaniards there content and willing to face the hardships of empire-building without some system of rewards? The settlers wanted their share of New World wealth, and this Spain accorded them, after she had taken out her "cut," the royal *quinto,* or fifth part. But there would have been no fifth, and no four-fifths, had there been no labor to mine the treasure. Whether rightfully or otherwise, the colonials felt that they must have the labor of the Indians, and the Crown yielded, trying all the while to give the Indians some official protection with laws and regulations.

Another question: Whatever the feelings of the Crown, could Spain have controlled her sons several thousand miles across the Atlantic more effectively than she did? Before attempting an answer to this, it might be well to recall the problems which faced the United States government in making its citizens on the frontier abide by treaty arrangements with the Indians of the American West.

Still another question: Did the American natives live completely without benefit under Spanish rule? Spain might have answered that they were initiated into the Christian faith, and occasionally they were. But were there other, more tangible benefits for the Indians?

This whole problem might seem to be something of an academic straw-man, set up to be knocked down by young historians. There may be elements of that, but its study has more far-reaching applications. Many of the practices which prevailed in the colonial centuries are basic to at least some of the inequities against which the Latin Americans are struggling today and which are so upsetting to established economy and society. These surviving traditions— not-so-subtle class distinctions, lack of enlightened interest in the welfare of the masses, actual peonage and related labor systems in some of the nations, and many more—do not square with modern democratic, or even Latin American quasi-democratic ideals. Though this study focuses on events and attitudes of centuries long gone, the problems which it describes are still with us. The Indian and the *casta* (the lower mixed-breed), in theory, have all the rights and privileges of citizenship in democratic states; but in practice—that is the proverbial "horse of another color."

The Conflict of Opinion

"The natives of the areas of the more advanced civilizations of the New World were far from unprepared for many aspects of the systems of tribute and services which their Spanish conquerors imposed upon them."

— ROBERT STONER CHAMBERLAIN

"I have a growing conviction that, in spite of the many absurdities committed in the name of religion and civilization, in the end the Council of the Indies and the rulers of New Spain worked out a way of life that was not intolerable and that the Spanish Utopia became not an unpleasant place in which to live."

— LESLIE BYRD SIMPSON

"Whereas, it has become evident through long experience that nothing has sufficed to bring the said chiefs and Indians to a knowledge of our Faith . . . , since by nature they are inclined to idleness and vice, and have no manner of virtue or doctrine . . . , and that the principal obstacle in the way of correcting their vices and having them profit and impressing them with the doctrine is that their dwellings are remote from the settlements of the Spaniards. . . . Therefore, . . . the said chiefs and Indians should be forthwith brought to dwell near the villages and communities of Spaniards. . . , so that they may be treated and taught and looked after as is right and as we have always desired; and so I command that henceforth that which is contained below be obeyed and observed. . . ."

— LAWS OF BURGOS

"Two ordinary and principal methods have the self-styled Christians, who have gone there, employed in extirpating these miserable nations and removing them from the face of the earth. The one, by unjust, cruel, and tyrannous wars. The other, by slaying all those who aspire to or sigh for or think of liberty or to escape from the torments that they suffer, such as all the native lords and adult men; for generally they leave none alive in the wars, except the young men and the women, whom they oppress with the hardest, most horrible, and roughest servitude, to which man or beast can be put. . . ."

— FRAY BARTOLOMÉ DE LAS CASAS

"It is not contrary to all this for the Crown to grant Indians in encomienda to the Spaniards. . . . From this, then, without going counter to the main aim, the conversion of the natives, flows a temporal good, namely, the preservation, the settlement, and protection of those lands and the governance and education of the Indians. Thus the Catholic faith is more fully served."

— ANTONIO RODRIGUEZ DE LEÓN PINELO

The fifth plague was the heavy tribute and services which the Indians rendered. . . . The sixth plague was the gold mines. . . . The Indian slaves who
up to the present have died in these mines cannot be counted. Gold, in this
land, was adored as a god in the form of a calf.

— MOTOLINÍA

"Would the New Laws have really benefited the Indians as much as Las
Casas believed, if the crown had stood firm against all the pressures to change
them? . . . We do know that the New Laws provoked the greatest battle of
the century, indeed of the whole colonial period, on Indian problems. . . .
It is also certain that the final decision of the crown to reverse itself and to
permit the encomienda to continue, not only terminated the fourth and last
experiment carried on by Spaniards during the first half-century of the conquest of America — it also terminated the period of experimentation in Indian
affairs."

— LEWIS HANKE

"[The repartimiento] is *illicito, y malo, y lleno de crueldad.*"

— FRANCISCAN MEMORIAL (1585)

"In the face of many obstacles the system of colonial labor progressed from
slavery, from unpaid personal services in lieu of tribute, from forced labor,
and from debt peonage, toward a standard of free paid labor, that is, toward
the economy common to the modern world . . . a social phenomenon manifestly of exceeding interest."

— SILVIO ZAVALA

"In Aztec society, labor had been prescribed and carefully regulated. . . . It is
evident that the native peoples of the conquest period were vulnerable to
the Spaniards' demands for labor. . . . Spaniards quickly took advantage of
the Indian attitude toward directed labor. . . . A major change under Spanish
rule, however, was that Indian peoples lost the sense of joyous participation
and adopted an attitude of resignation. . . . Labor tended thus to move from
the social, moral, and spiritual categories, in which Indians had placed it,
into the economic and physical categories of Europe."

— CHARLES GIBSON

PRE-CONQUEST LABOR PRACTICES

ROBERT STONER CHAMBERLAIN

Robert S. Chamberlain (1903–   ) holds a Bachelor of Arts degree from Stanford University and a Bachelor of Science from Ohio State University. His doctorate was earned at Harvard (1936). Most of his scholarly life has been spent in research with the Carnegie Institution of Washington, although he has taught briefly in several universities and on one occasion served as cultural relations officer for the American embassy in Guatemala. He has written on the conquest and colonization of Yucatan and Honduras. He also has a companion study to the one extracted here, in which he goes back to the mother country to find Castilian antecedents of the *encomienda-repartimiento*.

The following selection is intended to indicate that the labor-service-tribute system imposed by the conquistadores was not a wholly new thing to which the American Indians were subjected in post-conquest days. At least in the more developed civilizations the common folk long knew such exactions.

THE natives of the areas of the more advanced civilizations of the New World were far from unprepared for many aspects of the systems of tribute and services which their Spanish conquerors imposed on them. The question of the extent to which the Indians were prepared for these Spanish forms is not so much one of basic principles as of degree. The Indians gave tributes in various forms to their native lords and overlords and gave services to them and to the state and religion. Brought down to basic essentials, semi-feudal Spanish practices and native forms were comparable. The Spaniards recognized native institutions which were similar to their own when they arrived in the more highly developed areas of the New World, and the Indians on their part realized that certain institutions which the Spaniards established among them were basically like those they themselves had evolved.

The Spaniards naturally established in the New World the institutional forms with which they were familiar in Castile, evolving, adapting, and modifying them if necessary to meet the conditions they found in the overseas realms. In some cases Castilian institutions were from the first fused with already existing native political, economic and social forms, which, the Spaniards immediately perceived, were in essence like their own and like lingering feudal forms elsewhere in Europe. This was especially true with regard to the evolution of the repartimiento-encomienda system through which Spanish conquistadores and colonists were provided with rewards for their services and means to maintain themselves and their families.

The repartimiento-encomienda was one of the most significant of the institutions which the Spaniards evolved in the New World. The constitutional forms, usages, and customs on which this New World institution was based went far back into

From Robert S. Chamberlain, *The Pre-Conquest Tribute and Service System of the Maya as Preparation for the Spanish Repartimiento-Encomienda in Yucatan* (Miami, 1951), pp. 7–22, 27–31. Reprinted by permission of the University of Miami Press.

Castilian history where, over and above the institutions of the attenuated type of feudalism which existed in Castile, there were other unique forms and practices which grew out of the reconquest of Moorish lands in the Iberian Peninsula.

The terms *repartimiento* and *encomienda* are inseparably linked. *Repartimiento* had two meanings in its application to the *encomienda*: First, the act of division, or partition, of the Indians and native pueblos of a given area among the Spaniards upon its first conquest or occupation; and Second, the Indians or pueblos assigned in encomienda during the first partitition of a new region to *conquistadores,* or military conquerors, and *pobladores,* or first colonists who had not actually participated in the military operations. The Spaniard who received a grant of Indians or a native pueblo, or pueblos, under this system was an *encomendero.* As the institution became formalized under royal legislation, in the technical legal sense, Indians or pueblos assigned in the first partition of an area in repartimiento, in the meaning of the act of division, were *repartimientos.* They became *encomiendas* upon being assigned to a second encomendero following the death of the original grantee, or loss by him of his grant for cause stipulated by law. However, in practice, the term *repartimiento* in the sense of the Indians or pueblos assigned to encomenderos and the term *encomienda* were interchangeable in the earlier period.

The normal repartimiento and encomienda consisted of the right to enjoy the tributes, and until toward the mid-sixteenth century the labor services, of a designated number of Indians or of the inhabitants of specifically named pueblos, who were assigned to an encomendero as a reward for his services in the conquest and colonization of the region in which his repartimiento-encomienda lay. Until about the middle of the sixteenth century encomenderos could — entirely at their own will, and whenever they wished — fix the tributes and services which the encomienda Indians were to give them. This freedom of action

led to such great abuses and worked such hardships on the natives that the Crown first sought to legislate the eventual abolition of the encomienda system through the celebrated New Laws of 1542–1543, but this effort raised such a storm of protest throughout the Indies that the Crown had to give up the idea of eventual elimination of the system. Nevertheless the Crown began to impose more strict control over the institution and progressively formalized it through continuing legislation. Among the most important of these measures to bring the encomienda within the framework of royal government, some of which were begun even before the promulgation of the New Laws, were those which provided that Crown officials should establish fixed amounts and types of tributes for encomienda Indians and pueblos in accordance with population, activities of the natives, and resources of the area which they inhabited, and those designed to eliminate labor service of encomienda Indians for their encomendero. Tributes were now to be given only at specifically designated periods. Collection of tributes was henceforth either carried out by civil officials themselves, who assigned the encomenderos their return, or under the strict supervision of officers, who required the encomendero to limit collection to the amounts and types of tribute which had been fixed by official taxation.

The right to conduct repartimientos in the sense of the act of partition, and to assign Indians in encomienda, was an exclusive royal prerogative, since the natives of the New World were the direct vassals of the Crown of Castile. The sovereign delegated this prerogative to specifically designated high officials or superior agencies of colonial government, notably *audiencias,* who in turn could delegate power to specifically named lesser officials. Only with such authorization could Indians or pueblos be granted in repartimiento and encomienda. The official or organ of government empowered to grant repartimientos and encomiendas was obliged to issue titles, or cedulas of encomienda, to each encomendero. These titles clearly designated the Indians or pueblos involved in the grant. The encomendero was required to take formal possession of his repartimiento or encomienda, either in person or by proxy, in the presence of a duly authorized official. This ceremony was semi-feudal in nature. After the system was formalized, the assignment of encomiendas was not valid until the Crown itself, through the *Consejo de Indias* in Castile, highest organ of royal colonial government, had approved the grant.

The normal encomienda, that is the encomienda almost everywhere, involved no land tenure by the encomendero. The lands of encomienda Indians and pueblos remained in possession of the Indians themselves, whether as individuals or as a corporate body. This right was carefully safeguarded by the Crown to prevent encroachment by encomenderos on the lands of the Indians. Neither did the grant of a repartimiento or encomienda legally carry with it political authority or jurisdiction over his Indians or pueblos for the encomendero. Overlordship remained in the Crown alone.

The repartimiento-encomienda was not a perpetual grant, although a carefully regulated line of hereditary succession was established by the Crown. A grant was assigned for one, two, three and sometimes four lives after the institution was formalized, with renewal or confirmation of title by each successor a requirement. The Crown or other authorized officials could remove a repartimiento or encomienda from the encomendero at any time, but only for legally stipulated reasons, such as mistreatment of the natives, non-residence in the province in which the grant lay, failure to indoctrinate the Indians in Christianity, or failure to perform military service. Encomenderos throughout the Indies, both as individuals and as a caste, persistently sought to have their repartimientos and encomiendas turned into perpetual semi-feudal grants, carrying tenure of the land of their Indians and pueblos and political

jurisdiction, but the Crown refused to permit this transformation in the nature of the institution.

In return for the grant of a repartimiento or encomienda the encomendero was legally obliged to protect, and at his own expense to Christianize the natives assigned to him, and he was required by law to maintain arms and a horse in readiness to take the field at a moment's notice, whether against Indians, Spaniards who might rise up in rebellion, or European enemies who might attack the colonies. Women and minors who succeeded to encomiendas were obliged to maintain an *escudero,* or man trained to arms, for military service, since they themselves could not perform such duty. In this semi-feudal way the repartimiento-encomienda system provided a permanent militia throughout the Indies and was long the basis of the military system on which the overseas possessions of the Crown of Castile rested. Each city and town thus had its garrison, and periodic *alardes,* or musters and reviews, of the encomendero-militia were held. Every municipality was a garrison town, and its heavy government and ecclesiastical buildings made it also a fortress. In periods immediately following conquest, when there were many hardened veterans on hand, and on restless frontiers and in other areas where the colonists had to be constantly on the alert, the encomendero-militia had excellent combat value by any standard.

In effect the repartimiento-encomienda might almost be termed a money fief, if a loose feudal parallel is desired. As finally formalized by royal law, the repartimiento-encomienda was a right conferred by the Crown to enjoy the tributes of a designated number of Indians, or much more frequently, those of a specifically designated pueblo, or pueblos, with obligations on the part of the encomendero to Christianize the natives assigned to him and bring them to a higher state of civilization and welfare, and to perform military service.

If the repartimiento-encomienda is thought of as a kind of money fief, or perhaps, in another way, as a pension, it can readily be understood that the institution was of great importance to the conquistadores and original colonists of any given province. The repartimiento provided them with food and many articles which they needed for their daily lives, as well as surpluses which they could sell or trade for goods from Spain. Also, until the mid-sixteenth century the repartimiento-encomienda system legally provided the conquistadores and colonists with labor through which they could create and develop their *haciendas,* other holdings, and local industries. The encomenderos to a great extent maintained themselves and their households through their encomienda Indians. Therefore the winning of a repartimiento or encomienda grant was a matter of highest import to all conquistadores and pobladores, and conversely the removal of a repartimiento or encomienda was a matter of gravest financial consequences. Furthermore, almost all conquistadores served in conquests at their own cost, incurring great expenditures and indebtedness, hoping to gain compensation and further rewards in the subjugated lands. The repartimiento-encomienda was a principal means of obtaining lasting recompense for their arduous military services. It was also a means of providing reward to pobladores for their willingness to undergo the trials of colonization in new areas.

The Maya of Yucatan, as representatives of one of the highest of New World cultures, even though their civilization at the time the Spaniards first arrived in 1517 was by no means as brilliant as it had been during earlier periods, were among the natives who long had forms of tribute and service which prepared them for the imposition upon them of the repartimiento-encomienda system, and indeed for many Spanish government forms.

When the Spaniards discovered Yucatan and the Maya civilization in 1517 and began the long (and until 1540 halting) twenty-year conquest in 1527, the peninsula was divided into a number of independent native states, or *cacicazgos.* These independent states had come into being in the mid-fifteenth century after the overthrow of the tyranny of the Cocom family, who dominated northern Yucatan, and the destruction of their great capital Mayapan, following a bloody war against them led by the Xiu family. With the overthrow of the Cocom and Mayapan centralized authority disappeared and disintegration into separate territorial entities, each with its own ruling family, took place. The victorious Xiu became heads of the state of Mani and a Cocom survivor, traditionally the only one left, established the *cacicazgo* of Sotuta.

The independent states which the Maya formed were Acalán and Mazatlán in the southwest, Champotón, Canpech and Ah Canul on the west coast, Ceh Pech, Ah Kin Chel and Chikinchel on the north coast, and Ecab on the northeast coast. In the eastern interior were the Provinces of the Tazes, and the Cupul, with territory which extended to the north coast. Further west lay Sotuta and Mani, or Tutulxiu. In the interior of the northwest were Hocabá-Homún and Chakán. In the central interior was Cochuah, and south of it Uaymil-Chetumal, which extended to the Bay of Chetumal on the southeast. Far to the south, around Lake Peten, lay Tah Itzá, or Tayasal. Off the northeast coast was the island state of Cozumel.

All these states had well developed governments: some were centralized, or unitary, states; others were confederacies. Ralph L. Roys provides a succinct, authoritative description of the central and local governments of the Maya states as they were when the Spaniards came:

Many of the independent states were governed by a single ruler, and this dignitary was called the *halach uinic,* literally the "real man." We know that the Provinces of Mani, Sotuta, Ceh Pech, Hocaba, Cochuah, Champoton, and Cozumel had this form of government, and probably Ah Kin Chel, Tazes, and Tayasal also.

The halach uinic seems to have been primarily a war chief . . .

The office of halach uinic was confined to a certain family in each province where it existed: to the Xiu in Mani, the Cocom in Sotuta, the Pech in Ceh Pech, the Cochuah in the state that bore their name, and probably the Chel in Ah Kin Chel . . .

Besides acting as the local executive of the town which was his capital, the halach uinic formulated foreign policy and directed the government of his province through the local town heads, or batabs, many of whom were related to him. Although the batab usually acted as magistrate, serious cases (probably where more than one town was involved) were referred to the territorial ruler . . .

In addition to his political and judicial activities, the halach uinic evidently had certain definite religious functions as well . . .

No detailed description of what we might call the court of the halach uinic has come down to us. His household was no doubt similar to that of the batab but maintained on a larger scale, as he received tribute to live in considerable state . . .

The local town head was called the *batab*, who was appointed by the halach uinic in such provinces as we find the latter. A son usually succeeded his father to the position, if he was considered suitable, but in the Provinces of Ceh Pech and Mani many batabs were not sons of their predecessors. Where there was no halach uinic, the rules of succession were probably the same as those which governed the territorial ruler.

The batab's functions were administrative, judicial and military . . . In war the batab commanded the soldiers of the town, although there was a special war chief called the *nacom*.

The batab's power varied apparently in the different states. Where he was the appointee of the halach uinic, he was naturally subject to the orders of the ruler. If the province was a confederacy of independent towns, as in Ah Canul and probably in Chakan, the chief check on his authority was the ah cuch cabs, who were members of the council and without whose assent nothing could be done. In the Province of the Cupul were groups of towns, each dominated by the most powerful of the group. Although it is possible that this domination was confined to the exaction of tribute, I surmise that the authority of the subject batabs was limited by that of the ruling town . . .

The batab was treated with great ceremony and attended by many people when he went abroad. When he visited the house of one of his townsmen to drink, the populace accompanied him, bowing before him, opening a lane for him to pass, and spreading their mantles in front of him. Even on less ceremonious occasions they protected his head from the sun with great fans of bright feathers. . .

The members of the town council were the ah cuch cabs; they were also in charge of certain subdivisions of the town, collecting tribute and attending to other municipal affairs . . .

Another important official was the *holpop*, or *ah holpop*, whom the Spanish writers call overseer (*mandón*) and sometimes even a *cacique*.

In the same way Sylvanus G. Morley provides a statement of the position and labor services required of the common people:

The great mass of the people in both the Old and New Empires were humble corn farmers, whose sweat and toil supported not only themselves but also their supreme ruler (*the halach uinic*), their local lords (*the batabob*), and the priesthood (*ahkinob*). In addition to this no[t] inconsiderable task, they were the actual builders of the great ceremonial centers, the lofty pyramid temples, the vast colonnades, the palaces, monasteries, ball courts, dance platforms, terraces, and raised stone highways (Maya *Sacbeob*) which connected the principal cities. They likewise quarried, dressed, and sculptured the enormous quantities of stone and building blocks employed in these great constructions. They, with their stone axes, felled the thousands of trees which served for the fuel of the kilns where the local limestone was burned to make lime for the mortar, and with the same axes and stone-chisels they felled, fashioned, and carved the hardwood door lintels and roofbeams of sapodilla, the only wood that has been found in connection with Maya architecture. They were the masons, who dressed the building blocks, the stone workers who sculptured the stelae and carved the different elements in the elaborate stone-mosaic facades. And those same common folk were even beasts of burden who carried the stone from the quarries to the building sites, who climbed the pole scaffoldings, tied together with wild vines and lianas from the forest, carrying the heavy carved stone elements to their places, *on their own heads*.

The common people lived on the outskirts of the towns and villages: indeed, position in the social scale depended on the distance a man's house was from the central plaza of the city, town, or village where he lived.

It was this social class, by far the largest in the state, those lowly corn farmers, hewers of wood and drawers of water, these simple artisans, masons, stone cutters, carpenters, lime-burners, these carriers of burdens of every sort, who directed by the nobility but inspired by the priesthood, raised the great cities of stone that abound throughout the Yucatan Peninsula from the foothills of the cordillera in the far south to the shores of the Yucatan Channel in the far north — a prodigious human achievement.

Tributes and labor services were given by the common people to the halach uinic of unitary states, to the superior rulers in the case of confederacies, and in the case of at least one town to the batab. In the usual case the batab, assisted by the local officials, supervised the collection and delivery of tribute and the organization and carrying out of labor service.

Although the system of tributes of all Maya states and its administration were probably very similar, the amount of tribute required by various lords, and in different states, varied considerably. The information which has come down to us would seem to indicate that the amount of tribute required of the individual Indian by his native lord was moderate — even light — in most states, but that in total volume it was measurable. Over and above the tribute itself there was involved the labor and effort, whether in agriculture, weaving, gathering of salt, hunting, or fishing, which the individual tribute payer had to put forth to produce or gather it. In a number of instances it is declared that the tributes were not only light, but entirely voluntary, with the natives giving to their lords only what they wished, and from produce they had ready at hand. On the other hand, there are statements that some lords ruled absolutely and imposed their will in all

things as they saw fit, which does not correspond with the voluntary giving of tribute. In some cases it is emphasized that tribute was given only as token of recognition of the authority of the lord. On the other extreme, there is one statement that in one town natives who failed to pay tribute were sacrificed.

Tribute consisted of products of agriculture: maize, the great staple of the American Indian, beans, peppers; cotton products of the loom, cotton mantles, jackets, and "lesser clothing"; the return of hunting in the form of deer and peccaries; produce of fishing activity, and turkeys, honey, bees' wax, and *copal*, for incense. Salt, gathered from beds on the coasts, was another important item of tribute. In some instances highly prized shells, which the Indians used as money, and also greatly esteemed jade beads, were given in tribute. Service in the construction and repair of his houses was given to the halach uinic and superior rulers of confederacies, and service in the planting, cultivation of fields, and harvesting of crops for the lords was required. It seems likely that in certain instances such service was given to batabs also. Just as did the amounts of tributes, these services varied in extent for different lords and in different states. Military service was rigorously required by the lords.

The sixteenth century Franciscan missionary who became Bishop of Yucatan, Diego de Landa, in his celebrated *Relación de las Cosas de Yucatán*, has left us an excellent general statement of the system of tribute and labor service which existed among the Maya before the Spanish conquest:

The common people built at their own expense the houses of the lords . . . Beyond the house, all the town did their sowing for the nobles; they also cultivated them (the fields) and harvested what was necessary for him and his household. And when there was hunting or fishing, or when it was time to get their salt, they always gave the lord his share, since these things they always did as a community. If the lord died, although it was the oldest who succeeded him, the other children were very much respected and assisted and regarded as lords themselves. And they aided the other *principales* inferior to the lord in all these ways, according to who he was and the favor he enjoyed with his lord. The priests got their living from their offices and from offerings. The lords governed the town, settling disputes, ordering and settling the affairs of the republic, all of which they did by the hands of leading men, who were very well obeyed and highly esteemed, especially the rich, whom they visited, and they held court in their houses, where they settled their affairs and business usually at night. And if the lords went out of their town, they took with them a great many people, and it was the same way when they went out of their houses . . .

The Indians have the good habit of helping each other in all their labors. For the purpose of helping those who do not have their own people to do their work, they join together in groups of twenty, or more or less, and all together they do the work of all of them, (each doing) his assigned share, and they do not leave it until everyone's is done. The lands today are common property and so he who first occupies them becomes the possessor of them. They sow in a great number of places, so that if one part fails, another may supply its place . . .

They also join together for hunting in companies of fifty, more or less, and they roast the flesh of the deer on gridirons so that it shall not be wasted, and when they reach the town, they make presents to their lords and distribute the rest as among friends. And they do the same in fishing.

The origins of a system of tributes and service among the Maya remain lost in obscurity, but such a system must have been very old. Landa writes of the legendary Mexican prince Kukulcán, Toltec Quetzalcoatl, of the rise of the Cocom to power in Mayapán, traditionally founded by Kukulcán perhaps in the 10th century, and of a system of tribute which evolved:

After the departure of Kukulcan, the nobles agreed, in order that the government should endure, that the house of the Cocoms should have the chief power; because it was the most ancient or the richest family, or because at this time he who was the head of it was a man of the greatest worth. This being done, since within the enclosure there were only temples and houses for the lords and high priests, they ordered that other houses should be constructed outside, where each one of them could keep servants, and to which the people from their towns could repair, when they came to the city on business. Each one then established in these houses his mayordomo, who bore for his badge of office a short and thick stick, and they called him *caluac*. He kept account with the towns and with those who ruled them; and to them was sent notice of what was needed in the house of their lord, such as birds, maize, honey, salt, fish, game, cloth and other things, and the *caluac* always went to the house of his lord, in order to see what was wanted and to provide it immediately since his house was, as it were, the office of his lord.

The talented and educated Gaspar Antonio Chi, of the noble Xiu family, whose ancestors led the war against the Cocom and who was a court interpreter at the Spanish capital, Mérida, in the latter half of the sixteenth century, also wrote briefly of the system of tributes of the lords of Mayapán:

These lords of Mayapán held in subjection the entire (country, and) the natives of it were tributary (to them during the period when they ruled). The tribute (consisted of) small sheets of cotton, native hens, honey, (cacao and) a resin which served as incense in the temples and sacrifices (and in all) it was very little, in recognition of vassalage.

Another interesting account of the later evolution of a tribute system among the powerful and warlike Cupul of the area about present Valladolid is that of Juan Gutiérrez Piçón, encomendero of the town of Tiquibalán:

. . . The principal town of Tiquinbalón was called by this name by a great lord who was named Erbalam, which means Black Tiger, who was also called Cochcalbalán, which means 'Lord over All' . . . The (people) recognized Cochalbalán as lord, and he was the supreme one. The lords and captains (at first)

maintained them in justice . . . It is held to
be a strongly verified thing among the natives that they came from the direction of the
East with a great number of people, and having governed more than forty years, seeing
himself powerful and lord of many people, he
became proud and tyrannical, because he
deprecated his subjects and held them in low
regard and imposed unreasonable tributes on
them, and dealt with them unjustly in other
ways. This was the cause of his death, because
the common people conceived a great hatred
for him and (also) for his captains, because
they had become cruel. They took council
among themselves one day and killed them all.
As a result of his death there were immediately
many dissensions and deaths, because a great
part of his people felt aggrieved. It is said of
this lord and his captains that at the beginning
of his rule they were good and did not cause
grievances and that Cochcalbalán was a
sorcerer.

Because of the death of these lords Heblai-
chas, who was of their lineage, came to be
lord.

. . . As a result of the death of these Erba-
lanystas they raised a Copul to be lord, who
was a very celebrated lord. This Copul was
lord of Erbalán a long time and he governed
and maintained his province in justice and
was recognized and given tribute as such a lord.
(They) made him his planting of maize and
pepper, beans and cotton and other things for
his sustenance, and when it was necessary
they built him his house and repaired it . . .

An encomendero, Cristóbal Sánchez,
provides this general story of former unity,
disintegration, and the system of tribute
which existed during the earlier period of
unity:

At one time all this land was under the
dominion of one lord, who resided in the ancient city of Chichén Itzá, to whom all the
lords of this province were tributary. And
even from beyond this province, from Mexico,
Guatemala (Quahtemalin), Duapa (Chiapa?)
and other provinces they sent him presents in
sign of peace and friendship. And as time
passed, and Mayapán being peopled when a
lord named Tutulxiu made himself ruler and
as customs changed, . . . each province came
to have its own lords and caciques. Thus

when the conquistadores came to these provinces they found many lords and the provinces
divided. The tribute that they paid . . . was
a turkey hen each one, and some honey, and
some breadths (piernas) of mantles (paties),
and lesser clothing, although they served the
lords in person in wars when they occurred.

The Relación of the important town of
Motul, northeast of Mérida, provides one
of the best statements of the Maya tribute
system:

The dominion which these caciques and
lords held over their vassals was to hold them
subject to their will for whatever they wished;
and they obeyed them and regarded them with
greatest respect, providing them with whatever was necessary in time of peace, and aid-
ing them with their persons in war, without
the (lords' giving) them reward or pay. The
tribute which they gave them was cotton mantles, turkey cocks and hens, maize, honey, and
all other things in the nature of supplies and
clothing, because they did not have gold nor
silver, nor anything else of special value. But
from all that which the land produced they
gave of it to the governor in recognition of his
dominion.

The lords who governed took care to order
that the houses of their towns be constructed
and repaired, that . . . (the natives) make
their plantings of all products, and that in
their turns they work and cultivate them . . .

The Relación of Hernando de Braca-
monte, encomendero of Tequite, in the
Xiu territory south of Mérida, and an outstanding captain of the conquest period,
includes this statement, made after consulting Diego Xiu, cacique and governor of
his encomienda town, which indicates rigid
enforcement of tribute paying, in contrast
to many other declarations:

The oldest ones say that the land which
(makes up) these provinces was divided up
among many lords, and each one was lord of
the towns he held. Their subjects obeyed
these said lords . . . (and) gave tribute of that
which they had ready to hand, mantles, and
turkey hens and beans and dwarf red peppers
(axiaji), and slaves. And he who did not give
the tribute they ordered to be sacrificed.

The functions of the batab and the supervision of service by him are well illustrated by the organization of the town of Cinanche:

Their government, and that in general, was (in the hands of) lords, who were recognized as such, and whom they called *batabes,* which is the same as lords. These divided the town into its districts on the style of parishes and named a powerful and able man to have charge of each of them. They had care to present themselves with the tribute and service in their turns and to call together the people of their districts, both for banquets and celebrations, and for war, to which all, or the greater part of them went . . .

* * *

During the first years of the conquest the encomenderos of Yucatan, like those everywhere else in the Spanish Indies, required tribute and services of the Indians assigned them as they themselves saw fit, both with regard to kind and extent. In the latter 1540's however, when the conquest was finally completed, and as the Crown took increasing steps to bring the encomienda directly under royal control and under the machinery of colonial government, a fixed taxation of tributes was officially assessed. Begun about 1548 by the *Adelantado* Francisco de Montejo with the collaboration of Franciscan friars who came to the province, the taxation was completed by the *Audiencia* of Guatemala in 1552. This official taxation, which stipulated precisely the items of tribute each town should provide yearly, the amounts of each type of tribute to be given, and the times at which it should be given, was conscientiously intended to require of the natives only such products of agriculture, native industry, and fishing as the Indians were already accustomed to produce, and was adjusted to the numbers of the population, activities, and resources of each area and town. No encomendero was henceforth to require or receive tributes other than those officially established by the taxation.

The Crown intended that the tributes should be fair, equitable, and just, and carefully adjusted to the activities of the natives. The types of tributes and services given by the Indians to their native lords before the conquest were taken into consideration in establishing the official taxation. A royal *cédula* directing that such a taxation be made, issued to Montejo and the Bishop-Designate of Chiapas, Licenciado Juan de Arteaga, in 1540, well illustrates the purpose, intent, and fixed policy of the Crown in this regard:

Don Carlos, etc. To you, the Reverend in Christ Father Don Juan de Arteaga, Bishop of the province of Chiapas, and to our governor of that province and of the provinces of Yucatan and Cozumel, greetings. Know that we have been informed that because no assessment has been made of the tributes which the Indians of each town of those said provinces and diocese must pay, neither of those which the Crown Indians pay to us nor of those paid to the Spaniards who have held and hold Indians in encomienda, many things, and in larger quantities than the Indians should or can easily pay, have been and are collected from them. This has led and leads to many disadvantages which are very prejudicial to the nations of these provinces. This would cease if an assessment were made by our order and if the tributes each one must pay were known, for that amount and no more would be collected, either by our officials in the towns held in our name or by the Spaniards and private individuals who may hold them in encomienda or in any other manner. Experience has shown that since by our order the judges of our Audience which resides in the City of Mexico made an assessment of the tributes of New Spain the aforesaid evils and disadvantages have largely ceased (there). In order that henceforth they may also come to an end in those provinces of Chiapas, Yucatan, and Cozumel, and in those of that diocese, after discussion in our Council, it was recommended that we should issue this cedula to you in regard to this matter, and we approved.

Therefore we charge and order you that as soon as you see this, both of you (the bishop and the governor) acting jointly and in agreement, and neither one taking action alone, shall meet in the city of Ciudad Real. And when you have met, before doing anything further you shall hear a solemn mass of the Holy Spirit to enlighten your understanding and give you grace to perform well, justly, and legally what you will hereby be charged and ordered to do. After hearing the said mass you shall promise and solemnly swear before the officiating priest that you will do the things stated below well and faithfully, without enmity or favor. After this oath you, or the persons you may appoint for the purpose, who must be trustworthy and God-fearing, shall in the first place investigate the towns that are at peace in those provinces, both those held in our name and those granted in encomienda to conquistadores and colonists, and you shall ascertain the number of inhabitants and natives of each town and the nature of the land in which they live. You shall find out what they were accustomed to pay to their caciques and to the other persons who ruled and governed them in the past and what they now pay to the encomenderos, and what they can and should pay readily and without vexation now and henceforth to us and to the persons who, by our favor and will, may hold them in encomienda or in any other manner.

And after you are fully informed and, acting jointly and neither one without the other, have agreed on the amount of tribute that they should and can pay justly and readily as a token of submission to our authority, you shall state, tax and assess that amount according to God and your consciences, taking into consideration that the tributes they are thus to pay shall be in things they have or cultivate or that grow in their lands and districts, so that no imposition may be made the payment of which would lead to their ruin. After this (assessment) has been drawn up you shall make a census and inventory of the said pueblos and their inhabitants and of the tributes that you have thus assessed so that the said Indians may know that which it is that they must and are to pay and what our officials and the said encomenderos and other persons who may hold them by our order now and henceforth are to collect. You shall command them

on our behalf, and we now command and order them, that now and henceforth no official or private individual shall dare, publicly or secretly, directly or indirectly, in person or through a third party, to collect from the said Indians anything except what may be contained in your aforesaid taxation . . .

Under the fixed taxation of 1548–1552, the first in a series for Yucatan, the encomienda towns of that province were to provide their encomenderos with maize, cotton *mantas* (mantles), simple pottery, beans, peppers, cotton, wax, honey, fish, chickens (which were introduced early by the Spaniards), and similar products in proportion to their population and in accordance with their traditional activities, natural resources and geographical location. Mantles and the great Indian staple, maize, were principal articles of tribute, with beans another very important item. It will be recognized at once that many of these tributes required by the Spaniards were products which the natives gave to their own lords before the conquest. In the ultimate analysis, the encomendero and Spanish officials had merely replaced the Maya lords.

As population and other factors changed, other official taxations were made later in what the Crown intended should be fair adjustments to new circumstances. There seems no doubt, however, that the tributes required by the Spaniards were much heavier than those demanded or received by the Maya lords before the conquest.

From all we know of the tribute and service system of the Maya, as illustrated by information available from existing sources, it seems clear that the natives of Yucatan were far from unprepared for the repartimiento-encomienda system which the Spaniards imposed on them.

SPANISH UTOPIA

LESLEY BYRD SIMPSON

Lesley Byrd Simpson (1891–   ), although born in Missouri, has been identified with the University of California for so many years that it would be difficult to think of him as other than a Californian. His teaching field, until his retirement in the middle 1950's, was Spanish literature. His special interest, and very productive research field, has been the institutional history of New Spain. Over the years he has become one of the foremost interpreters of Spanish-Indian relationships during the colonial centuries. Some of his studies on this and related topics are listed in the "Suggestions for Additional Reading" at the end of this volume.

The present piece is an excellent overview of the problem which this volume proposes for study and discussion, putting the topic in historical setting and passing a not unsympathetic verdict on the labor system. Simpson's later studies have not greatly modified this view.

THE ambitious task I have set myself to accomplish is to lay before you in outline the history of an amazing experiment — the story of the heroic and quixotic ideal which Spain once so stubbornly pursued in this hemisphere. That ideal was nothing less than to set up in the New World a City of God — a very Spanish City of God.

When Spain found her way to Asia blocked by an enormous and impassable body of land, teeming with a population of every degree of development, she was willy-nilly presented with a vast sociological laboratory in which to experiment as she pleased. It was inevitable, given the highly religious and nationalistic character of their long crusade against the Moors, that the Spaniards should seek to impose upon the New World the burning ideals of that crusade: one God, one king, one creed, one way of life — the Spanish.

We were once taught to look upon the Spanish adventure in America as a haphazard, aimless, and brutal business. Like all conquests, that of the Spaniards was certainly brutal at times, and their social experiment was generally muddle-headed and haphazard, but aimless it was not. I shall try to present their aims and ideals realistically and to describe the organic institutions that evolved in the conflict of those aims and those ideals with the realities of existence in this unfriendly hemisphere.

The concept of an ideal Christian society based upon the imperative mode had for centuries been the plaything of theologians. This was especially true of the Spanish rulers during the great period of discovery. The impact of that imperative upon the New World dates from the time of Columbus. One might say that Columbus himself was the first utopian of the New World, although, to be sure, he never learned that he had discovered a New World. For his great dream was to launch a last Crusade against the infidel — to take the Saracens in the rear, so to speak, to restore the Holy

A research lecture delivered in Berkeley, March 3, 1937, under the auspices of the Graduate Division of the University of California and published in *Hispania*, XX (1937), pp. 353–368. Reprinted by permission of *Hispania*.

11

Land to christendom, to add the dominions of Mohammed and their revenues to the Spanish crown. Columbus died in the belief that he had embarked Spain upon that project, but by the time of his death it was apparent to every one else that a great and useless continent lay between Spain and her Asiatic ambitions. Never, it is safe to state, was a magnificent discovery more unwelcome to its makers.

An obliging papacy presented the new lands to the crown of Castile, under the solemn agreement that their inhabitants were to be made Christians. That famous pact was more or less justly scoffed at by interested foreigners as a hypocritical pretext for a piece of high-handed robbery. Nevertheless, as the magnitude of the new territories and their unbaptized millions became known, the legal minds of the Council of the Indies earnestly set to work to devise some means of converting the peoples of this hemisphere into God-fearing and tax-paying Spanish subjects. We are apt, here in California, to look upon those two functions, political and religious, as fundamentally at odds with each other, as was the case here during the period of the missions. Such a development was, perhaps, inevitable, but nothing could have been farther from the intent of the framers of the Spanish utopia in the Council of the Indies. Priest or layman, conquistador or missionary, the responsibility was the same: to bring the heathen to Christ and their ducats to the Spanish treasury.

That utopia, that Spanish heaven-on-earth, as first conceived, was a belated and fumbling attempt to christianize and civilize the unlucky inhabitants of the greater Antilles, but, before anything constructive could be done, the distressing realities of the situation bade fair to destroy Spaniard and Indian alike.

But we must begin at the beginning. Columbus, on his return to Spain in 1493, wrote the first real estate prospectus of America. "There are in that island," he wrote, "mountains and valleys and fields, and beautiful fat lands for planting and sowing, for raising cattle of all kinds, for cities and villages. The ports are such that you would not believe them without seeing them, as are the many and great rivers of sweet waters, most of which are gold-bearing. . . . The people all go naked, as their mothers bore them, save only that some of the women cover a single part with a green leaf, or a cotton cloth made for the purpose. They have no iron or steel or arms; nor are they apt for such things, not because they are not well set-up and beautiful, but because they are wonderfully timorous. . . . They are so guileless and so liberal with what they have that you would not believe it without seeing it."

Small wonder that Columbus had no difficulty in enlisting a regular horde of adventurers (some fifteen hundred of them) to go with him to this new Eden. But one important essential had been overlooked, namely, the food supply. The natives of the Antilles had got along well enough on a diet of manioc bread (our tapioca), but they planted only enough for their own needs. The hungry Spaniards ate all the manioc, and Spaniards and natives were soon reduced to the verge of starvation. The problem of procuring food was immediate and the situation was heavy with disaster. "Nothing in those days," wrote Las Casas, "gladdened the people here more than to learn that ships were coming with supplies from Castile, for all their troubles were from hunger." The quest for food, as I shall have occasion to repeat many times, was the greatest and most continuous modifying factor in all Spanish plans for setting up their commonwealth in America. Starvation, indeed, accounted for fully half of the entire Spanish population of the New World during those tragic thirty years, up to the discovery of Mexico. Conditions became so hideous that the colony of Española could be kept up only by shipments of convicts. "Indeed," wrote Oviedo, "I saw many of those who at that time returned to Castile with such faces that I think that although the King had given me his Indies, were I to become as they, I should not have gone thither."

Now, the cultivation of manioc is extremely laborious, although the yield is generous. The jungle must be grubbed up, hillocks built, the weeds kept down. Then the manioc root must be harvested, grated, and the poisonous juice squeezed out — after which the flour is made into a heavy flat cake. Manioc was such an important item in the Spanish invasion of America that it is hardly too much to say that the New World was conquered on manioc.

The aversion of the Spanish conquistadores (and others) to manual labor in the tropics is notorious, and the new parasite class insisted on being fed and made rich. The problem was a simple one. What were the natives for if not to work for their new masters? So the Indians were forced to plant manioc and wash gold, and were kept so unremittingly at it and with so little regard for their strength and habits that the major part of the population of Española and the surrounding islands died off in the first twenty years. But the Spaniards had not been sent to the Indies merely to eat soggy manioc bread and sluice gravel for gold. Back in the Council of the Indies were those who remembered that they were on the last Great Crusade and that these natives were part of the swarms of unbelievers who must be made over into Spanish Christians and tax-payers. The paradox of saving the souls of the heathen, while using their bodies for profit, agitated the legal minds of the Council for many years, and was solved only after a bitter struggle which brought on a furious civil war and which came perilously close to destroying the Spanish Empire. But I am anticipating.

In the early days of Española the matter was settled summarily by recourse to a proposition which may be rather baldly stated as follows: "Is it not just to make the Indians work for the Spaniards in exchange for the ineffable gifts of Christianity and the profit system?" Lest this proposition should shock you, let me add that one of the most persistent criticisms directed by the Spaniards against the Indians was that they had no sense of values: that they would not work for wages, and that they exchanged things of great price for things of little price. All of which, of course, strikes one as the flimsiest sort of rationalization. However, acting upon it (and driven by the present specter of hunger), Columbus and his followers ground the natives under a stupid and brutal exploitation, for which one can hardly find a parallel outside the Belgian Congo of the past century. When the despairing islanders resisted, well, they were obstinate heathen rebels and could legally be enslaved. It was the shiploads of Indian slaves sent back to Spain by Bartholomew Columbus that excited the wrath of Queen Isabella and first brought home to her and her Council the urgency of doing something about redeeming their pledge.

So out of starvation, slavery, and death, came the first New Deal to America. It was entrusted to Don Nicholás de Ovando, Lord Commander of the military order of Calatrava. He was sent out to Española in 1502 to save the colony from the effects of the disastrous mismanagement of the Columbus brothers: to suppress Indian and Spanish rebels, and to restore order. The stern old commander was equal to the task. Within a year the Indians (those who were left alive) had been thoroughly subdued, as well as those turbulent spirits among the Spaniards whom Columbus had signally failed to govern. But Ovando, like all his successors, still had to face the double problem of feeding the population and of converting the Indians into Christians and Spanish subjects. He it was who introduced the much-discussed system of *encomiendas* (trusteeships, or guardianships) by which the Moorish provinces of Spain had been administered. Under his system the natives were divided into lots of varying sizes (depending upon the category of the recipient) and these lots (*encomiendas*) were put under the tutelage of presumably God-fearing and high-minded Spanish laymen. It is well to remember that this was long before the establishment of religious missions. The *encomendero* was, in fact, a lay missionary, as well as a collector of the tribute and general overlord of the Indians. According to the theory, by his Christian example and teaching the Indians were to be induced to accept the godly life, after the European pattern of the fifteenth century. It was the new citizens' obligation, naturally, to pay taxes for the support of the state, and, since they had no money with which to pay them, it was clearly their duty to work them out by raising manioc and washing gold. This legal fiction, invented by Columbus and formalized by Ovando, became in time the principle underlying the entire economic structure of Spanish America. The Spaniard of 1500 saw no essential contradiction between destroying a man's body and saving his soul. The body, indeed, was frequently destroyed for that single purpose.

The invention of the *encomienda* was the first halting step in the setting up of a stable commonwealth in America. Whatever its immediate and practical motives were, the *encomienda* made the Great Crusade the layman's responsibility. It need not astonish us that the *encomendero* took that responsibility lightly. The early Spaniards of Española were so intent upon procuring the necessities of life that the new legal fiction made no difference whatever in their treatment of the Indians. By 1510 conditions among the miserable remnants of the population of Española were such that the first Dominican missionaries to arrive there were horrified. Looking for an easy answer to the universal desolation they thought they had found it in the *encomienda*, and they set to work at once and vigorously on their long campaign for its abolition. Their protests to the Council of the Indies brought about a tardy and, in some respects, ludicrous attempt to save the situation: the Code of Burgos of 1512. This famous code, the first written for the

Western Hemisphere, is an excellent example of that irrationality, idealism, and almost total ignorance, characteristic of those early Spanish clergymen who ruled the New World. Lack of space prevents a discussion of the astonishing measures they thought necessary for the government of a subject race. One of them, for example, provided for teaching the natives to say their prayers in Latin; another restricted their sinful and heathenish habit of taking baths. Several principles, however, were laid down which became a permanent part of the legal structure of the Indies. The first of these was, of course, that the inescapable and most important duty of the Spanish crown and the colonists was to convert the Indians to Christianity and to bring them to a "reasonable" way of life. In spite of Dominican protests, the *encomienda* was retained as an instrument to that end. Second, and of enormous importance for the subsequent history of America, the Code of Burgos postulated the necessity of organizing the natives into regular European communities, in which they would live under Spanish tutelage and in which their services would be more available.

The Code of Burgos was far from satisfactory to the Dominicans, who were already beginning to argue that the Spaniards were merely interlopers in the New World and had not the shadow of a right to the land, goods, and labor of the Indians. Their most effective mouthpiece was the famous cleric, Bartolomé de las Casas, who was sent to Spain in 1516 to lobby for them. The plan he presented was typical for its other-worldliness and complete impracticality. It called for the abolition of the *encomienda*, the restitution of all Indian property, the prohibition of all forced services, and the setting up of a colonial government composed entirely of ecclesiastics, whose first and almost single duty should be the conversion and protection of the natives. Las Casas did not lay the plan before the Council (which had passed the wicked Code of Burgos), but hastened to

King Ferdinand himself. That weary monarch, however, evaded the issue by dying, leaving as regent of Castile Cardinal Ximénez de Cisneros. The cardinal was one of the greatest statesmen of his day, yet such was the power of Las Casas' argument, and such the weight of theological prestige, that he was persuaded to give the plan a trial. Nothing could have been more quixotic and nothing more certain of immediate collapse. Yet Cisneros forced the plan through the Council of the Indies and three ancient and holy friars of the Jeronymite order were dragged, protesting, from their cells and sent across the sea to administer the new heaven-on-earth. After Las Casas' departure, however, Cisneros had an attack of common sense and issued secret instructions to the effect that if the difficulties encountered proved insurmountable the friars were to leave things as they were.

Things turned out as he had anticipated: the obstacles encountered were certainly insurmountable and, to the towering wrath of Las Casas, things were left much as before.

The other-worldliness of the Council of the Indies hardly needs another illustration, but I cannot resist the temptation to add one more. Las Casas, disgusted, fretting, and fulminating denunciations against the unfortunate Jeronymites for their betrayal of his great scheme, hastened once again to Spain to pour his wrath into the ear of Cardinal Cisneros, but that aging statesman was weary of Las Casas' importunations and refused to interfere with the Jeronymites. Thereupon Las Casas despaired of saving the vanishing islanders from the devil and the Spaniards. Instead, he turned his remarkable energies into a new project, which he dinned at the Council for the next three years. The incredible result was that the Council granted him an immense tract of land in South America, roughly equal in area to all the United States east of the Mississippi. Upon that land Las Casas contracted to plant settlements of honest and God-fearing Spanish peasants, *who would do their own work,* and who, by their example and teaching, would lead the aborigines to God. It was an idealized *encomienda.* Not only did he convince the Council of the plan's feasibility, but he managed to enlist some two hundred peasants in his Salvation Army. Fifty of these men, who contributed a hundred ducats apiece for the privilege, were appointed as leaders. Las Casas dubbed them his "Knights of the Golden Spur" and gave them a white robe with a red cross on the breast to distinguish them from their humbler fellows. The company was assembled at Seville in 1520 under the immediate command of its treasurer. That worthy, however, embarked with the company and all the funds, without waiting for Las Casas, and they were lost to history in the wilds of Puerto Rico. Somebody was always betraying Las Casas. Nothing daunted, he recruited another Band of Hope and embarked with it the next year for Cumaná (on the Pearl Coast, near the mouth of the Orinoco), expecting to pick up the first company in Puerto Rico. Alas! Enthusiasm for the godly life soon evaporates in the tropics, and the new evangelists went the way of their predecessors. Las Casas reached his empire finally with five men and two priests. Leaving them at Cumaná to set up his first model community, he sailed for Santo Domingo to get more men, only to be met by news that the Caribs had descended upon Cumaná and butchered his whole company.

The foregoing episode has little importance in itself. It does, however, illustrate the magnificent and child-like optimism of the learned theologians of the Council of the Indies, whose faith in the efficacy of written plans, laws, and high-sounding professions was never completely lost. It is significant that the councils of the world's greatest empire were for centuries dominated by medieval theologians, who clung to their ideal long after it had become hopelessly apparent that that ideal was unworkable.

Thus matters stood in the Indies when word came of the stupendous discovery of the empire of Mexico by Cortez. Cortez, in his turn, became the most effective realtor in America. With his account of the new land of milk, honey, and easy wealth, a fresh swarm of adventurers descended upon this hemisphere, and a new impulse was given to the utopia-makers of the Council of the Indies. The frightful extermination of the population of the Antilles had had its effect, and the Council determined that no such fate should overtake the Kingdom of New Spain. The *encomienda*, which was still mistakenly blamed for all the ills of the Indies, was forbidden, but, by the time the decree reached New Spain, a large part of that land had been divided among the conquerors in traditional style. It was profoundly contrary to Hapsburg political philosophy to perpetuate this illegitimate offspring of feudalism, and the Council put all the remaining towns of New Spain under royal magistrates (*corregidores*), who were paid a salary and who were directly responsible to the crown.

The *corregidores* were necessarily chosen from among those later comers to the Indies, men who had arrived too late to participate in the first spoils of conquest. It may be stated generally that all Spanish laymen came to the Indies to improve their fortunes. The corregidor's salary of a few hundred pesos a year fell far short of the riches he had dreamt of. It was inevitable, then, that a considerable number of these magistrates should use their great powers to line their pockets at the expense of the Indians. Petty graft, extortion, and forced labor at once became so general among them that the Kingdom of New Spain was threatened with the same fate that had overtaken the islands.

Exploitation of the Indians continued, but strong checks were now present. The Indians of New Spain were not the delicate and primitive race that had peopled the islands. They were hardy and inured to the exacting labor of agriculture. Moreover, the missionaries were now numerous and powerful and were bound, from motives of self-interest and religious conviction, to protect the Indians. They were unremitting in their protests against exploitation. Their agitation bore fruit in 1542. Under the presidency of the Dominican Cardinal Loaysa, the Council of the Indies made another attempt to codify the relations between Indian and Spaniard. The new code was known as the *New Laws of the Indies for the Good Treatment and Preservation of the Indians*. As the title indicates, the purpose was the same as that of the Code of Burgos, and the Council now had more experience behind it. With characteristic lack of realism, however, the Council detroyed the only means that had been developed for supporting life in the colonies, namely, slavery, forced services, and the *encomienda*. Protests immediately poured in from every hand, all repeating the same argument, that life in the colonies was impossible without the labor of the Indians. But not until a disastrous civil war had broken out in Peru did the Council modify the objectionable clauses. Humanitarian historians have condemned the Council of the Indies for thus retreating from its high stand, but I submit that it could do nothing else. The New Laws did, however, definitely limit the power of the colonists to exploit the labor of the Indians without interference, and the principles then established became the permanent law of the Indies.

I hardly need repeat again that all measures which aimed at the amelioration of the Indians broke against the hard necessity of procuring food and labor. It is still an unfathomable mystery that the Council could not envisage that fundamental problem until it had brought the colonies to the brink of chaos. The *encomendero*, the *corregidor*, the priest, the missionary, the miner, the farmer — all Spaniards, in short — were forced to enter into a tacit conspiracy to defeat the idealism of the Council.

In the New Laws of 1542 the Council defined the Indians as free subjects of the King of Spain. Less formally, the colonists defined them as lazy, improvident, childish, irresponsible, drunken vagabonds — a definition which has persisted to this day and which, better than any commentary, reflects the profound gulf between Indian and European cultures.

Clause XXVI of the New Laws abolished "all forced labor of free Indians," and that clause was never repealed. To take the place of forced services the Council, with unconscious humor, proposed the use of Negro slaves, and of paid free labor. But Negro slaves were expensive and troublesome, and the Indians had no tradition of, and no interest in, working for wages. So the government was faced once again with the old problem of finding means of getting necessary work done and of procuring food. Out of this necessity issued an invention, admirable in its ingenuity, by which the Indian, "without sacrificing his liberty," could be forced to assume the obligations of citizenship, as his masters understood them. The new invention was the *repartimiento*.

The *repartimiento* rested upon the now familiar premise that the state may force its citizens to perform those tasks that are necessary for its existence. In this case such tasks were defined as the operation of farms and mines, the erection of public buildings, churches and convents, the opening and maintenance of roads, harbors, and irrigation ditches, the laying out of new towns, and the care of travelers. In a word, there were few mechanical tasks which were not necessary for the support of the commonwealth. But the important and revolutionary thing about the new set-up was that all such services must be paid for in cash. Furthermore, the *repartimiento* was regarded by the Council as a necessary evil at best, a temporary makeshift, and was only to be tolerated until such time as the Indians should have learned to work for wages. It was meant as a sort of educational interlude. But it lasted for almost three centuries, and its logical successor, peonage, is still going on under one guise or another.

It is highly probable that the new system was looked upon by the colonists merely as a subterfuge, an evasion of the ugly word "slavery," and the wages paid strike one as illusory. Nevertheless, the insistence upon the principle of paid labor marked an immense advance in the status of the Indian. The *repartimiento* once having been legalized, it became necessary, especially in agriculture. It became, in fact, the economic base of agriculture throughout the Spanish Empire in America. So great was its importance and so profound its effect upon the social and economic pattern that I must discuss it in some detail.

Under the system of *repartimientos* a percentage of the male population of any village between the ages of eighteen and sixty could be called upon to work for wages on some specific task for a week or a fortnight. The percentage varied from four to seven per cent in the mines to twenty-five per cent in agriculture. A Spaniard desiring the services of Indians made out a regular application, to the effect that he was engaged in the production of wheat, corn, or cattle, or that he operated a mine, or wished to erect a church — all for the good of the commonwealth — and that he needed the services of so many Indians for such a length of time. He agreed to pay them the prevailing wages and to treat them well. There is a lively description of the operation of the system written by that amusing scoundrel, Thomas Gage, who was in New Spain and Guatemala from 1625 to 1637. It is worth quoting.

"The Spaniards who live about that country," he wrote, "allege that all their trading and farming is for the good of the commonwealth, and therefore whereas there are not Spaniards enough for so ample and large a country to do all their work, and all are not able to buy slaves and black-amoors, they stand in need of the Indians' help to serve them for their pay and hire; whereupon it hath been considered that a partition of Indian labourers be made every Monday, or Sunday in the afternoon, to the Spaniards, according to the farms they occupy. . . . So that for such and such a district there is named an officer, who is called *juez repartidor*, who, according to a list made of every farm, house, and person, is to give so many Indians by the week. . . . They name the town and place of their meeting upon Sunday or Monday, to the which themselves and the Spaniards of that district do resort. The Indians of the several towns are to have in a readiness so many labourers as the Court of Guatemala hath appointed to be weekly taken out of such a town, who are conducted by an Indian officer to the town of general meeting; and when they come thither with their tools, . . . with their provision of victuals for a week, . . . and with their beds on their backs, . . . then are they shut up in the townhouse, some with blows, some with spurnings, some with boxes on the ear, if presently they go not in.

"Now all being gathered together, and the house filled with them, the *juez repartidor,* or officer, calls by the order of the list such and such a Spaniard, and also calls out of the house so many Indians as by the Court are commanded to be given unto him, and delivereth unto the Spaniard his Indians, and so to all the rest, until they be all served. . . . If complaint be made by any Spaniard that such and such an Indian did run away from him, and served him not the week past, the Indian must be brought and surely tied by his hands to a post in the market-place and there be whipped upon his bare back. But if the poor Indian complain that the Spaniard cozened and cheated him out of his shovel, axe, bill, mantle, or wages, no justice shall be executed against the cheating Spaniard, neither shall the Indian be righted, though it is true that order runs equally in favour of both Indian and Spaniard. Thus are the poor Indians sold . . . for a whole week's slavery, not permitted to go home at nights unto their wives, though their work lie not above a mile from the town where they live; nay, some are carried ten or twelve miles from their home, who must not return till Saturday night late, and must that week do whatsoever their master pleaseth to command them. The wages appointed them will scarce find them meat and drink, for they are not allowed a real a day, which is but sixpence."

Although the *repartimiento* was subject to abuse, I cannot completely share Thomas Gage's indignation (which, I suspect, was not entirely sincere). Relatively speaking, the Indian under the *repartimiento* was in no worse plight than the contemporary European peasant, and, as the *repartimiento* became regulated by custom, he may even have been better off. It was certainly not slavery, and was infinitely to be preferred to what had gone before.

Several factors combined to make the *repartimiento* tolerable. The most important factor, possibly, was the constantly recurring shortage of labor. The Spanish population of New Spain increased rapidly and its demands for labor became progressively more insistent. The Indian population, on the other hand, decreased with even greater speed, that is, up to the end of the sixteenth century. Smallpox, measles, typhus, and alcohol reduced the numbers of the natives alarmingly, until there were not enough left to do the work. The situation was analogous to that of Europe during the Black Death of the fourteenth century. In the mines especially the competition for Indian labor early raised wages to a scandalous height. The constant demand for labor in the mines and the need for skilled and specialized mechanics ended by putting the mines on a free labor basis. The condition of the Indian miner in Mexico by 1803 was so enviable that it caused Humboldt to exclaim: "The labour of a miner is entirely free throughout the whole kingdom of New Spain. . . . The Mexican miner is the best paid of all miners."

Although the *repartimiento* persisted in agriculture, the same forces were at work there as in the mines, and wages show a gradual increase until they reached a peso a week — not a princely figure, to be sure, but then it should be borne in mind that the Indian in the country did not depend on wages for his living. His only fixed expenses were the tribute, which came to a peso and a half a year, and his contributions to the church. He was obliged to give twelve weeks out of the year to the *repartimiento,* and the rest of the time was his own. The system was extraordinarily easygoing, compared with any other forced labor system of my acquaintance, and it was frightfully inefficient, very likely, but under it the native population flourished and increased prodigiously.

Nor was the Indian left without powerful protection. The first viceroy of New Spain, the great Antonio de Mendoza, inaugurated the custom of devoting one day a week to the hearing of Indian complaints and to meting out summary justice. The policy was continued by his successors until, by 1575, the volume of business had grown so large that a special court was created to handle Indian cases alone. This extraordinary court, the Juzgado General de Indios, functioned with the authority of the Supreme Court of New Spain. It was so remarkable and so original an institution, and its stabilizing effect so enduring, that I must beg your indulgence for a short description of it.

The Juzgado was composed of the viceroy himself, two or three judges of the Supreme Court, and a state's attorney. This latter officer was paid by the state (out of Indian tributes) to brief, present, and argue the Indians' cases. An interpreter was also provided by the state. Every effort seems to have been made to prevent unnecessary expense to the Indian complainant. Private lawyers were not allowed to represent them. Most admirable of all was the rule that Indian cases had to be heard and settled on the same day. I have examined all the extant records of the Juzgado de Indios, some 35,000 folios, which cover a period of 250 years. The cases deal with every conceivable source of friction between Spaniard and Indian. Altogether they make a sordid chronicle of petty thievery, extortion, peonage, rape, false imprisonment, beating, and brutality generally, which could hardly be duplicated outside the police records of our own cities. But, to my utter astonishment, after a careful scrutiny of the innumerable cases, I failed to find more than one which was decided against the Indian complainant. After some reflection, however, my amazement was moderated, because it was evident that only the exceptionally strong cases could ever hope to reach that high court, while the infinity of lesser cases were settled, justly or unjustly, by the local magistrates. Nevertheless, the Juzgado de Indios was a humane and practical instrument for reducing the inevitable friction between the two strata of society.

How effective was it? Well, it was accessible only to those Indians who could reach it, and, in a territory as vast as that of New Spain, a great part of the population was far too remote to have any immediate recourse to the Juzgado. Yet, the very existence of such a court, the immense number of cases it heard, and the penalties it imposed, could hardly fail to have their effect. The bitter denunciations of it voiced by the magistrates of the lower courts for its undermining of their authority are good evidence that its labors were felt, deeply, in some cases. I recollect, for example, one instance in which the offenders, a group of miners, were deprived of Indian labor for ten years — which meant that they were forced out of business.

The Juzgado de Indios, then, was an effective device for carrying out the will of the Council of the Indies, perhaps the only effective one where the Indians were concerned. I suggest that the long generations of peace enjoyed by that most fortunate of Spanish colonies may be explained as much by the patriarchal activities of the Juzgado de Indios as by the superior arms of the Spaniards. It is sad to reflect that this admirable instrument was not invented by the zealous utopians of the Council of the Indies, but by the hard-headed viceroys of New Spain, who had to solve a difficult problem in practical politics.

There remains for discussion the profound change in political and community life among the Indians of New Spain directly traceable to the interference of the Council of the Indies. You will remember that the Council had recognized from the beginning that the Indians must be brought into organized communities before any lasting change could be made in their habits. It is no accident that wherever one goes in the ancient Spanish Empire one sees the uniform imprint of the Spanish town builders. The physical and political structure of the Indian village of today is a close replica of the sixteenth-century Spanish community. How did this come about?

Characteristically, without taking into account the magnitude of cost of the undertaking, the Council of the Indies, from the time of the Code of Burgos of 1512, never ceased from insisting upon the congregation of the Indians into organized communities. After the conquest of New Spain this insistence became progressively sharper. Each viceroy, upon assuming office, was reminded of that necessity. The viceroys evaded the issue for half a century, appalled at the cost and difficulty of the undertaking. They pleaded lack of funds, insufficient personnel, inadequate knowledge of the country, damage to the Indians, possible rebellion. But the Council and the order-loving Hapsburgs would not be gainsaid, and the instructions of Viceroy Luis de Velasco II, in 1590, ordered him to undertake at once the congregation of the Indians. His instructions were minute. Each new village was to be laid out in rectangles, with a square, a church, a jail, a community house, wide streets, building lots, and the rest. The townsite was to be selected by experts with an eye to its salubrity, water supply, communications, and an abundance of arable land. Each village was to be governed by its own elected Indian officers (with, of course, the advice of the priest). Significant in the light of what is happening in Mexico today was the inalienable tract of land attached to each village — the *ejido*. In short, the plan for the congregation of the Indians reflected the sixteenth-century Spanish ideal of village life. I confess to some admiration of it myself.

Don Luis took his instructions seriously.

Like his royal master, Philip II, he had a naïve confidence in the efficacy of the imperative mode. Getting together a hundred commissions, composed of a judge, a notary, and a constable each, he armed them with the indispensable sealing-wax and sent them far and wide to locate townsites. A mighty protest went up on all sides, from priest, missionary, *hacendado,* and Indian alike. The congregation went ahead nevertheless. The cries of distress reached the Council of the Indies. The viceroy was destroying the country; the Indians were suffering cruelly; they were about to rebel; and so on. By way of reply the Council sent out a new viceroy, the Count of Monterey, to complete the colossal task. The Count applied himself to it, in the face of determined opposition. The cost was great, in money and suffering, but the congregation was not abandoned. It is unfortunate that the records of that extraordinary enterprise have largely perished, but enough remain to give us a notion of its scope. It embraced the territory, roughly speaking, of the old Aztec empire; that is, most of the land lying south of the twenty-second parallel, and a good bit north of it. The congregation was limited in the main to the sedentary agricultural Indians, although some villages were established which included considerable groups of nomads — *chichimecas,* as they were called. All the evidence at my disposal leads me to believe that the congregation was generally successful, because very many of the towns are identifiable today. The policy of congregating the Indians of New Spain was continued up to the very end of the Spanish régime. By that time most of the Indians of New Spain were living in Spanish communities, governing themselves more or less according to Spanish law, and worshipping, after their fashion, a Spanish God.

The utopia-makers of the Council of the Indies (fortunately, perhaps) failed to realize completely their City of God in the New World, although those reverend gentlemen, with unparalleled stubbornness, persisted for centuries in their quixotic attempt to make reality out of a purely literary concept. Among the manifest difficulties they failed to envisage was the rise of an immense and troublesome new class, the half-castes, out of which came the ferment which today is destroying the last vestiges of the Spanish Utopia. The members of the Council seem not to have had the remotest notion of the social organism that was taking shape beyond their ken, and it was a cause of perpetual bewilderment to them that their carefully thought-out plans uniformly went wrong, or were changed into something very different from the original intent. And yet, though their plans were continually destroyed or modified by unforeseen or ignored circumstances, I find in their real accomplishments something of a challenge to the materialistic interpretation of history. Chief among these accomplishments was the consistent and generally benevolent supervision which the Council exercised over native life, and it did so when, materially speaking, it would have been enormously more profitable to let events take their course. Consider, for instance, the liberation of some 300,000 Indian slaves back in 1550, when it meant ruin to great numbers of Spaniards and a heavy loss to the crown, and all because the Council had decided that it was unethical to enslave innocent heathen. Negroes, evidently, were not innocent heathen. The benevolent effect of that supervision becomes immediately apparent when one contemplates by way of contrast the miserable plight of the Indians of Mexico during the first century of independence, for, deprived of the protection of the Spanish crown, they were thrown back into a state of hopeless servitude, from which only now they are beginning to emerge.

My Mexican friends argue that Spain fastened upon their unhappy land a medieval concept of life, a false social pattern unsuited to it, an oppressive and wasteful economy, a demoralizing caste system. In a word, according to them, Spain was the author of all the ills that beset Mexico today. One must agree with a great deal of that indictment. And yet, when I look back upon New Spain of the late eighteenth century, when colonial life had settled into a comfortable old age, I am not appalled by those things. The master-and-servant division of society is insulting to a vigorous democracy, but one should remember that neither Spaniard nor Indian had ever heard of "liberty, equality, and fraternity," and it seems silly to condemn them for living the sort of life that fitted the habits of both groups. So I have a growing conviction that, in spite of the many absurdities committed in the name of religion and civilization, in the end the Council of the Indies and the rulers of New Spain worked out a way of life that was not intolerable and that the Spanish Utopia became not an unpleasant place in which to live.

THE LAWS OF BURGOS

THE CROWN OF SPAIN

As an example of Spanish legislation, its phraseology, and general pattern of expression, the Laws of Burgos are here reproduced in full, along with the Amendments of 1513. They have been called the first formal code of laws which sought to regularize the relationships of the conquistadores and their new subjects. The Crown tried to provide against the abuses which had shown in Española and against which the Dominican friars, notably Antonio de Montesinos and Pedro de Córdoba, had begun to campaign so vigorously. Later these prescriptions came under the wrathful fire of Fray Bartolomé de Las Casas, who labeled them "iniquitous, cruel, tyrannical, and contrary to natural law . . . impossible . . . irrational and worse than barbarous."

Whereas, the King [Doña Juana] my Lord and Father, and the Queen, my Mistress and Mother (may she rest in glory!), always desired that the chiefs and Indians of the Island of Española be brought to a knowledge of our Holy Catholic Faith, and, *Whereas,* they commanded that certain ordinances be drawn up, which were indeed drawn up, by their Highnesses, as well as, at their command, by the Comendador Bobadilla and the Comendador Mayor de Alcántara [Ovando], former governors, of the said Island, and afterward by Don Diego Columbus, our Admiral, Viceroy, and Governor of it, and by our officers who reside there, and, *Whereas,* it has become evident through long experience that nothing has sufficed to bring the said chiefs and Indians to a knowledge of our Faith (necessary for their salvation), since by nature they are inclined to idleness and vice, and have no manner of virtue or doctrine (by which Our Lord is disserved), and that the principal obstacle in the way of correcting their vices and having them profit by and impressing them with the doctrine is that their dwellings are remote from the settlements of the Spaniards who go hence to reside in the said Island, because, although at the time the Indians go to serve them they are indoctrinated in and taught the things of our Faith, after serving they return to their dwellings where, because of the distance and their own evil inclinations, they immediately forget what they have been taught and go back to their customary idleness and vice, and when they come to serve again they are as new in the doctrine as they were at the beginning, because, although the Spaniard who accompanies them to their village, as is there ordered, reminds them of it and reprehends them, they, having no fear of him, do not profit by it and tell him to leave them in idleness, since that is their reason for returning to their said village, and that their only purpose and desire is to do with themselves what they will, without regard for any virtue, and, *Whereas,* this is contrary to our Faith, and, *Whereas,* it is our duty to seek a remedy for it in every way possible, it was considered by the King, my Lord and Father, and by several members of my Council and by

Reprinted from *The Laws of Burgos of 1512–1513: Royal Ordinances for the Good Government and Treatment of the Indians,* translated, with an introduction and notes, by Lesley Byrd Simpson (San Francisco, 1960), pp. 11–47, by permission of John Howell—Books.

persons of good life, letters, and conscience, and they, having informed themselves from others who had much knowledge and experience of the affairs of the said Island, and of the life and customs of the said Indians, gave it as their opinion that the most beneficial thing that could be done at present would be to remove the said chiefs and Indians to the vicinity of the villages and communities of the Spaniards — this for many considerations — and thus, by continual association with them, as well as by attendance at church on feast days to hear Mass and the divine offices, and by observing the conduct of the Spaniards, as well as the preparation and care that the Spaniards will display in demonstrating and teaching them, while they are together, the things of our Holy Catholic Faith, it is clear that they will the sooner learn them and, having learned them, will not forget them as they do now. And if some Indian should fall sick he will be quickly succored and treated, and thus the lives of many, with the help of Our Lord, will be saved who now die because no one knows they are sick; and all will be spared the hardship of coming and going, which will be a great relief to them, because their dwellings are now so remote from the Spanish communities, so that those who now die from sickness and hunger on the journey, and who do not receive the sacraments which as Christians they are obligated to receive, will not die [unshriven], because they will be given the sacraments in the said communities as soon as they fall sick; and infants will be baptized at birth; and all will serve with less hardship to themselves and with greater profit to the Spaniards, because they will be with them more continually; and the visitors who have them in charge will visit them better and more frequently and will have them provided with everything they need, and will not permit their wives and daughters to be taken from them, as now happens while they live at a distance; and many other evils and hardships will cease which the Indians now suffer because they are so remote, and which are not described here because they are notorious; and many other advantages will accrue to them for the salvation of their souls, as well as for the profit and utility of their persons and the conservation of their lives; and so,

Therefore, for these reasons and for many others that could be adduced, it was agreed that for the improvement and remedy of all the aforesaid, the said chiefs and Indians should forthwith be brought to dwell near the villages and communities of the Spaniards who inhabit that Island, so that they may be treated and taught and looked after as is right and as we have always desired; and so I command that henceforth that which is contained below be obeyed and observed, as follows:

I

First, since it is our determination to remove the said Indians and have them dwell near the Spaniards, we order and command that the persons to whom the said Indians are given, or shall be given, in encomienda, shall at once and forthwith build, for every fifty Indians, four lodges [*bohíos*] of thirty by fifteen feet, and have the Indians plant 5,000 hillocks (3,000 in cassava and 2,000 in yams), 250 pepper plants, and 50 cotton plants, and so on in like manner, increasing or decreasing the amount according to the number of Indians they have in encomienda, and these shall be settled next the estates of the Spaniards who have them in encomienda, well situated and housed, and under the eyes of you, our said Admiral and judges and officers, and of our visitor who will be in charge of it, or of the person whom you, our said Admiral and judges and officers, shall send for the aforesaid purpose, and he, I charge and command you, shall be such as will be competent in this matter; and the persons who have the said Indians in their charge [in encomienda] shall have them sow, in season, half a *fanega* of maize, and shall also give them a dozen hens and a cock to raise and enjoy the fruit thereof, the chickens as well as the eggs; and as soon as the Indians are brought to the estates they shall be given all the aforesaid as their own property; and the person whom you send for this purpose shall tell them it is for their own use and that it is given them in exchange for what they are leaving behind, to enjoy as their own property. And we command that the persons to whom they are given in encomienda shall keep it for them so that they may enjoy it as their own; and we command that this property shall not be sold or taken from them by any person to whom they may be given in encomienda, or by anyone else, but that it shall belong to the said Indians to whom it is assigned and to their descendants, even though this said person sell the estate in which they are, or the said Indians be removed from him; and we declare and command that the person to whom the said Indians are given in encomienda may utilize the goods that the said Indians abandon when they are brought to the estates of the Spaniards, each according to the number of Indians he has, in order to maintain them with such goods; and after the said persons have removed the said goods I command you, our said Admiral and judges and officers, to have the lodges of the said villages burned, since the Indians will have no further use for them: this so that they will have no reason to return whence they have been brought.

II

After the aforesaid has been done, we order and command that all the chiefs and Indians dwelling on the Island of Española, now or in the future, shall be brought from their present dwelling places to the villages and communities of the Spaniards who reside, now or in the future, on the said Island; and in order that they be brought of their own volition and suffer no harm from the removal, we hereby command Don Diego Columbus, our Admiral, Viceroy, and Governor of the said Island, and our appellate judges and officers of it, to have them brought in the manner that seems best, with the least possible harm to the said chiefs and Indians, to this end encouraging them and urging them with praise; and we charge and command them most earnestly to do this with much care, fidelity, and diligence, with greater regard for the good treatment and conservation of the said Indians than for any other respect, desire, or interest, particular or general.

III

Also, we order and command that the citizen to whom the said Indians are given in encomienda shall, upon the land that is assigned to him, be obliged to erect a structure to be used for a church, on a site selected by you, the said Admiral, judges, and officers, or by the visitor appointed by you; and in this said church he shall place an image of Our Lady and a bell with which to call the Indians to prayer; and the person who has them in encomienda shall be obliged to have them called by the bell at nightfall and go with them to the said church, and have them cross themselves and bless themselves, and together recite the *Ave Maria*, the *Pater Noster*, the *Credo*, and the *Salve Regina*, in such wise that all of them shall hear the said person, and the said person hear them, so that he may know who is performing well and who ill, and correct the one who is wrong; and since the period we command to be allowed them for rest before nightfall is principally for the purpose of having them rested at the hour of evening prayer, in case any Indian should fail to come to the said church at the said time, we command that on the day following he shall not be allowed to rest during the said period; but he shall still be urged to go to prayers the next night; and we also command that each morning, before they go to work, they shall be obliged to go to the said church and pray as they do in the evening; but they shall not be obliged on that account to rise earlier than is customary, that is, at full daylight.

IV

Also, in order to discover how each one is progressing in things of the Faith, we command that every two weeks the said person who has them in charge shall examine them to see what each one knows particularly and to teach them what they do not know; and he shall also teach them the Ten Commandments and the Seven Deadly Sins and the Articles of the Faith, that is, to those he thinks have the capacity and ability to learn them; but all this shall be done with great love and gentleness; and the person who fails to obey this shall incur a penalty of six gold pesos, two of which shall be for our treasury, two for his accuser, and two for the judge who sentences him and executes the sentence; and I command that the penalty shall be executed at once upon the persons of those who incur it.

V

Also, because I have been informed that the Spaniards and Indians who live on the estates go for a long time without hearing Mass, and since it is right that they should hear it, at least on feast days and Sundays, and since it is impossible for each estate to maintain a priest to say Mass, we order and command that where four or five estates, more or less, are within the distance of a league, on that estate which is nearest the others a church shall be built, and in this church an image of Our Lady and a bell shall be placed, so that every Sunday and obligatory feast day they may come there to pray and hear Mass, and also to hear the good advice that the priests who say Mass shall give them; and the priests who say Mass shall teach them the Commandments and the Articles of the Faith, and the other things of the Christian doctrine. Therefore, in order that they be instructed in the things of the Faith and become accustomed to pray and hear Mass, we command that the Spaniards who are on the estates with the said Indians and have charge of them shall be obliged to bring them all together to the said church in the morning and remain with them until after Mass is said; and after Mass they shall bring them back to the estates and give them their pots of cooked meat, in such wise that they eat on that day better than on any other day of the week, and, although the priest who says Mass will sometimes be absent, nevertheless they shall bring them even so to the church to pray and receive good advice. If, however, the other estates are in places where the Indians can easily come to hear Mass, the said citizens shall be obliged to bring them thither, on pain that any person who has charge of the said Indians and fails to bring them [to Mass] shall incur a penalty of ten gold pesos: six pesos as prescribed in the preceding article, and of the four remaining, two shall be for the erection of the said church and two for the priest who teaches the Indians.

VI

Also, since it is our will that the best means be sought to persuade the Indians to accept the things of our Holy Catholic Faith, and since if they should have to travel more than a league to hear Mass on Sundays and feast days it would be a grave hardship for them, we order and command that, if beyond the aforesaid league where we command the said church to be built there should be other estates, even though they should be in the same district, a church shall be erected there in the aforesaid manner.

VII

Also, we order and command the prelates and priests who, now and in the future, collect the tithes from the estates where the said Indians are, to maintain priests continually in the said churches of the said estates, to say masses on Sundays and obligatory feast days; and [we order and command] also that the said priests shall have charge of confessing those who know how to confess, and of teaching those who do not. Thus Our Lord will be served, and, if the contrary is done, He has been and will be disserved.

VIII

Also, we order and command that at the mines where there are a sufficient number of Indians churches shall be built, in convenient places approved by you, our said Admiral, judges, and officers, or by the person selected by you, so that all the Indians who are at the mines may hear Mass on the said feast days; and we command the settlers and Spaniards who bring the said Indians to extract gold, to observe with them the same procedure that is followed on the estates, as prescribed above, under the same penalties applied in the same manner.

IX

Also, we order and command that whoever has fifty Indians or more in encomienda shall be obliged to have a boy (the one he considers most able) taught to read and write, and the things of our Faith, so that he may later teach the said Indians, because the Indians will more readily accept what he says than what the Spaniards and settlers tell them; and if the said person has a hundred Indians or more he shall have two boys taught as prescribed; and if the person who has Indians does not have them taught as ordered, we command that the visitor who in our name has charge shall have them taught at the cost of such person. And because the King, my Lord and Father, and I have been informed that several persons are employing Indian boys as pages, we order and command that the person who does so shall be obliged to teach them to read and write, and all the other things that have been prescribed above; and if he fails to do so the boys shall be taken from him and given to another, because the principal aim and desire of the said King, my Lord and Father, and mine, is that in the said parts and in each one of them our Holy Catholic Faith shall be planted and deeply rooted, so that the souls of the said Indians may be saved.

X

Also, we order and command that each and every time an Indian falls sick in a place where there is a priest, the priest shall be obliged to go to him and recite the *Credo* and other profitable things of our Holy Catholic Faith, and, if the Indian should know how to confess, he shall confess him, without charging him any fee for it; and, because there are some Indians who already understand the things of our Holy Faith, we command that the said priests shall be obliged to have them confess once a year, and also that they shall go with a Cross to the Indians who die and shall bury them, without charging any fee for it or for the confession; and if the said Indians die on the estates we command that the Christian settlers there shall bury them in the churches of the said estates; and if they die in other places where there are no churches they shall be buried where it seems best, on pain that he who has Indians in his charge and fails to bury them or have them buried, shall pay four gold pesos, which shall be applied and distributed in the following manner: one for our treasury, one for his accuser, one for the judge who sentences him, and one for the priest at the estate or village where the said Indians are buried.

XI

Also, we order and command that no person having Indians in encomienda, or any other person, shall use Indians as carriers for transporting supplies to Indians at the mines, but that when the latter are removed from one place to another they shall carry their own effects and provisions, because we have been informed that there are no beasts of burden there; and the aforesaid is to be observed and obeyed, on pain that the person who employs the said Indians as carriers against the tenor and form of this article shall pay, for each offense, two gold pesos, which shall be for the hospital of the village where the said settler lives; and if the burden which he thus puts on the Indians is of foodstuffs, he shall lose it also and it shall go to the said hospital.

XII

Also, we order and command that all the Spanish inhabitants and settlers who have

Indians in encomienda shall be obliged to have all infants baptized within a week of their birth, or before, if it is necessary; and if there is no priest to do so, the person who has charge of the said estate shall be obliged to baptize them, according to the custom in such emergencies, on pain that he who fails to obey this article shall incur, for each offense, the penalty of three gold pesos, which we command shall be for the church where the said infants are baptized.

XIII

Also, we order and command that, after the Indians have been brought to the estates, all the founding [of gold] that henceforth is done on the said Island shall be done in the manner prescribed below: that is, the said persons who have Indians in encomienda shall extract gold with them for five months in the year and, at the end of these five months, the said Indians shall rest forty days, and the day they cease their labor of extracting gold shall be noted on a certificate, which shall be given to the miners who go to the mines; and upon the day thus designated all the Indians shall be released in the district where the founding is to be done, so that all the Indians of each district shall go to their houses on the same day to rest during the said forty days; and in all the said forty days no one shall employ any Indians in extracting gold, unless it is a slave, on pain that for every Indian that any person brings to the mines in the said period of forty days shall pay half a gold peso, applied in the aforesaid manner; and we command that in the said forty days you, the said officers, shall be obliged to finish the founding. And we command that the Indians who thus leave the mines shall not, during the said forty days, be ordered to do anything whatever, save to plant the hillocks necessary for their subsistence that season; and the persons who have the said Indians in encomienda shall be obliged, during these forty days of rest, to indoctrinate them in the things of our Faith more than on the other days, because they will have the opportunity and means to do so.

XIV

Also, since we have been informed that if the Indians are not allowed to perform their customary dance [*areytos*] they will receive great harm, we order and command that they shall not be prevented from performing their dances on Sundays and feast days, and also on work days, if they do not on that account neglect their usual work stint.

XV

Also, since the most important consideration for the good treatment and increase of the Indians is their subsistence, we order and command that all persons who have Indians shall be obliged to maintain those who are on their estates and there to keep continually a sufficiency of bread and yams and peppers, and, at least on Sundays and feast days, to give them dishes of cooked meat, as is prescribed in the article that says that on feast days when they go to Mass they shall be given better pots of meat than on other days; and on the days when meat is to be given to the Indians of the said estates it shall be given them in the same manner as is prescribed for the Indians at the mines; that is, they shall be given bread and peppers and a pound of meat a day, and on feast days fish or sardines or other things for their subsistence; and those who are on the estates shall be allowed to go to their lodges to eat, on pain that the person who has the said Indians and does not fulfill all the aforesaid contained in this article shall incur for each offense the penalty of two gold pesos, which shall be distributed as prescribed above; and if he should be fined three times and still fail to correct himself, at the fourth conviction the Indians he has in encomienda shall be taken from him and given to another.

XVI

Also, we order and command that, among the other things of our Faith that shall be taught to the Indians, they shall be made to understand that they may not have more than one wife at a time, nor may they abandon her; and if the persons who have them in encomienda see that they have sufficient discretion and knowledge to undertake matrimony and govern their households, they shall procure their lawful marriage, as our Holy Mother Church commands, with the wife of their choice; and we especially command that the chiefs be made to understand that they may not take wives related to them, and we command that the visitors shall be responsible for their understanding this, repeating it to them very frequently and telling them, or having them told, all the reasons for their so doing, and how by this action they will save their souls.

XVII

Also, we order and command that now and in the future all the sons of chiefs of the said Island, of the age of thirteen or under, shall be given to the friars of the Order of St. Francis who may reside on the said Island, as the King my Lord has commanded in one of his decrees, so that the said friars may teach them to read and write, and all the other things of our Holy Catholic Faith; and they shall keep them for four years and then return them to the persons who have them in encomienda, so that these sons of chiefs may teach the said Indians, for the Indians will accept it more readily from them; and if the said chiefs should have two sons they shall give one to the said friars, and the other we command shall be the one who is to be taught by the person who has him in encomienda.

XVIII

Also, we order and command that no pregnant woman, after the fourth month, shall be sent to the mines, or made to plant hillocks, but shall be kept on the estates and utilized in household tasks, such as making bread, cooking, and weeding; and after she bears her child she shall nurse it until it is three years old, and in all this time she shall not be sent to the mines, or made to plant hillocks, or used in anything else that will harm the infant, on pain that the person who has Indians in encomienda and fails to obey this shall, for the first offense, incur the penalty of six gold pesos, distributed as prescribed above, and for the second offense the woman and her infant shall be taken from him, and for the third, the woman and her husband and six other Indians.

XIX

Also, we order and command that all those on the said Island who have Indians in encomienda, now or in the future, shall be obliged to give to each of them a hammock in which to sleep continually; and they shall not allow them to sleep on the ground, as hitherto they have been doing; and they shall give them this hammock within the twelve months immediately following their receiving the said Indians in encomienda. And we command our visitors carefully to observe whether each Indian has the said hammock, and to urge the said persons who have them in encomienda, if they have not already supplied hammocks, to do so within the said following twelve months, [on pain that the person who fails to obey the aforesaid shall incur the penalty of . . . pesos], and this penalty we command you, our said Admiral and judges, to execute on the person who incurs it. And since it is said that when anything is given to an Indian he immediately wishes to exchange it for something else, we command that the said Indians be admonished by the visitors that they are not to exchange the said hammocks for other things, and if they do exchange them, we command the said visitors to punish the Indians who do so and to void the exchanges they have made.

XX

Also, we order and command that, in order that henceforth the Indians may have wherewith the better to clothe and adorn themselves, the person who has them in encomienda shall give to each of them a gold peso every year, which he shall be obliged to give them in wearing apparel, in the sight of and with the consent of our visitor, and this gold peso shall be understood to be in addition to the said hammock that we commanded above to be given to each of them. And since it is just that the said chiefs and their wives should be better dressed and better treated than the other Indians, we command that one *real* be deducted from the gold peso to be paid to the latter, and that with this said *real* the said visitor shall have clothing purchased for the said chiefs and their wives; and we command you, our said Admiral, judges, and officers, to have special care to see that this article is observed, obeyed, and fulfilled.

XXI

Also, in order that each one may employ only the Indians he has in encomienda, and that no one may employ those belonging to another, we order and command that no person or persons shall employ an Indian belonging to another, or receive him in his house or estate or mine, or anywhere; but if an Indian should be traveling from one place to another, we permit him to be detained for one night on an estate, provided that immediately on the following morning he is sent forth to go and serve his master; and we command that the person who fails to obey this, and detains an Indian not given to him in encomienda, shall incur the penalty for the loss of one Indian of his own for every Indian of another he thus detains; and the said Indian shall be given to the accuser and the other returned to his master; and if the said person has no Indians he shall suffer the penalty, for the first offense, of six gold *castellanos*; for the second, twelve; and for the third the penalty shall be doubled again and distributed in the prescribed manner; and if he has no Indians or money the penalty shall be commuted to one hundred lashes.

XXII

Also, we order and command that, in order that the chiefs may the more easily have people to serve them in their personal needs (provided that the Indians of the said chiefs are distributed among more than one

person), if a chief has forty subjects two of them shall be given to him for his service; if he has seventy he shall be given three; if a hundred, four; from a hundred to a hundred and fifty, six; and from that point onward, even though he should have more subjects, he shall not be given more; and these said Indians who are to serve him shall be chosen by the said chief, provided they are man and wife and child; and we command that the said Indians shall be chosen from among those belonging to the person who has the largest share of the subjects of the said chief in encomienda. And we command that they [the said chiefs] shall be well treated and not forced to work save at light tasks, so that they may be occupied and not idle, thus avoiding the difficulties that might arise from idleness. And we command our visitors to look carefully after the said chiefs and Indians, and to feed them well and teach them the things of our Holy Faith better than they teach the others, because [the said chiefs] will be able to indoctrinate the other Indians, who will accept it more readily from them.

XXIII

Also, we order and command that all persons who have in encomienda Indians of the said Island of Española, as well as those brought from other islands, shall be obliged to give an accounting to the visitors, within ten days, of those who die and those who are born; and we command that the said visitors shall be obliged to keep a book in which to enter every person who has Indians in encomienda, and the Indians that each one has, with their names, so that those who are born may be entered, and those who die removed, and the visitor have continually a complete record of the increase or decrease of the said Indians, on pain of two pesos gold for each offense, levied against each of the said settlers who fails to do so; and this penalty shall be divided among the treasury and the accuser and the judge who sentences him; and the visitors shall be obliged to bring to each founding an account of all the aforesaid and give it to our officers there, so that they may know how much the Indians have increased or decreased between one founding and the next, and they shall so inform us when they remit us the gold that falls to our share in the said founding.

XXIV

Also, we order and command that no person or persons shall dare to beat any Indian with sticks, or whip him, or call him dog, or address him by any name other than his proper name alone; and if an Indian should deserve to be punished for something he has done, the said person having him in charge shall bring him to the visitor for punishment, on pain that the person who violates this article shall pay, for every time he beats or whips an Indian or Indians, five pesos gold; and if he he should call an Indian dog, or address him by any name other than his own, he shall pay one gold peso, to be distributed in the manner stated.

XXV

Also, since we have been informed that many persons having Indians in encomienda employ them in commerce or trade, thereby disserving us, we order and command that each person having Indians in encomienda shall be obliged to bring the third part of them to the mines to extract gold, or more than the third part if he so desires, on pain that if he fails to observe this he shall incur a penalty of three gold pesos for each Indian lacking in the said third part to be sent to the mines; but we permit the residents of La Sabana and Villanueva de Yaquimo to be excused from bringing Indians to the mines, because of their remoteness; but we command them to employ the said Indians in the manufacture of hammocks and cotton shirts, in raising pigs, and in other activities profitable to the community. And whereas I have learned that when the Indians are removed to the estates of the settlers it is necessary to employ some of them at once in the erection of lodges, and in other tasks that the settlers will indicate to them as required for their estates, and because of which they will not immediately be able to send the third part to the mines, I command you, the said Admiral, judges, and officers, forthwith to fix for all this the period you think should be allowed, making it as brief as possible.

XXVI

Also, we order and command that those who have Indians [in encomienda], but whose estates are so remote from the mines that they cannot supply provisions for the said Indians [being sent thither], shall combine their Indians with those of others who have estates in the vicinity, in order to supply provisions for the said Indians, one person supplying the provisions and the other the Indians, provided that the master of the Indians [being sent to the mines] sends along with them a miner who will see to it that they do not lack necessities; and the aforesaid shall not be done through a third party, or in any way other than that prescribed, under the penalty stated above.

XXVII

Also, since many Indians have been brought, and are daily being brought, from the neighboring islands, we order and command that these said Indians be indoctrinated in and taught the things of the Faith, in the form and manner that we have commanded to be observed with the other Indians of the said Island; also, that they shall be inspected by the said visitors, unless they are slaves, for these may be treated by their owner as he pleases; but we command that they shall not be treated with that rigor and harshness with which other slaves are customarily treated, but rather with much love and gentleness, in order the better to incline them to the things of our Faith.

XXVIII

Also, we order and command that each and every time any person vacates the Indians he has in encomienda, either by death or for some other reason for which he may deserve to lose them, the person to whom we grant the said estate in encomienda shall be obliged to purchase it from the one who has vacated the said Indians, or from his heirs, and it shall be appraised under oath by two persons who are acquainted with it, to be named by you, the said Admiral, judges, and officers; and the said owner shall be obliged to sell it at their appraisal, so that the said Indians do not have to change their residence, because the persons to whom they are given [in encomienda] must be residents of the community to which the said Indians were allotted.

XXIX

Also, we order and command that in each community of the said Island there shall be two visitors in charge of inspecting the whole community, together with its mines and estates, its shepherds and swineherds, and they shall ascertain how the Indians are being taught in the things of our Faith, and how their persons are being treated, and how they are being maintained, and how they or the persons who have them in charge are obeying and fulfilling these our ordinances, and all the other things that each of them is obliged to do; and we command them to have particular care in all this, and we charge their consciences with it.

XXX

Also, we order and command that the said visitors shall be selected and named by you, the said Admiral, judges, and officers, in the form and manner you think best, provided they are selected from among the oldest inhabitants of the communities in which they are to serve; and we command that they shall be given and assigned some Indians in encomienda, in addition to those given them for their responsibility and work in the use and exercise of the said office; and these Indians shall be chosen by you, the said Admiral, judges, and officers; and it is our will that if the said visitors should become negligent in enforcing the said ordinances, or if any of them fail to carry out the aforesaid, especially in the matter of subsistence and hammocks, their own Indians that they have in encomienda shall on that account be removed from them.

XXXI

Also, we order and command that the said visitors shall be obliged twice a year to inspect all the places where there are Indians of their charge, once at the beginning of the year, and again at the middle; and we command that one of them alone shall not make the inspection both times, but each one once, so that each may know what the other is doing and so that everything may be done with the necessary care and diligence.

XXXII

Also, we order and command that no visitor shall bring to his house or estate any lost or runaway Indians he finds in the estates or elsewhere, but that immediately upon finding them he shall deposit them with a person of good conscience whom he shall select; but first he shall endeavor to discover who their master is, and when he has done so he shall deliver the Indians to him at once; otherwise, they shall be deposited as prescribed until the said master is found, on pain that the visitor who is discovered with an Indian in his possession or in his house shall lose an Indian of his own, to be given to his accuser, and the said runaway Indian taken by the visitor shall be restored to his master.

XXXIII

Also, we order and command that the said visitors shall be obliged to have and keep in their possession a copy of these our ordinances, signed by the said Admiral, judges, and officers, together with the instructions that we command you, the said Admiral, judges, and officers, to give them, by which they may the better know what they must do, observe, and obey; and upon the visitor who fails to obey, the aforesaid penalties shall be executed.

XXXIV

Also, we order and command that you, the said Admiral, judges, and officers, shall inquire once every two years into the way in which the said visitors are fulfilling their duties, and you shall have their *residencias* taken, in which it shall be ascertained how they have enforced these ordinances, each according to his obligation. And we command that the said visitors shall be obliged, at the time of their residencias, to give you, the said Admiral, judges, and officers, a very complete accounting of all the Indians and their number, each reporting for the place in his charge, and how many have been born and how many have died in those two years, so that the said Admiral, judges, and officers may send us an accounting of it all, which shall be signed by you and the visitors, to the end that I may be well informed of everything.

XXXV

Also, we order and command that no inhabitant or resident of the said communities of the said Island of Española, or of any other island, shall have in encomienda, by grant or otherwise, more than a hundred and fifty Indians, or fewer than forty.
Therefore, I command you, our said Admiral, judges, and officers, and each and every one of you, present and future, and all other persons whatsoever to whom the contents of these ordinances may apply, to consider the ordinances incorporated above and those others mentioned, and to observe and obey them, and to have them observed and obeyed and executed completely, each according to its contents; and you shall execute and cause to be executed the penalties upon such as incur them; and also, you shall observe and obey the said ordinances yourselves, according to the manner and form prescribed therein, under the penalties stated. Moreover, in case of disobedience, you shall incur the loss of the Indians you have in encomienda, and they shall be considered vacated, so that we may assign them to whomsoever we please; and you shall not act counter to their tenor and form, nor shall you permit them to be violated at any time or in any way. And if, in order to fulfill and execute the aforesaid, you should have need of favor and aid, I hereby command all town councils, justices, regidores, knights, squires, officers, and citizens of the said Island of Española to render you such favor and aid as you shall demand of them, under whatever penalties that you in our name shall impose, which by these presents I impose and consider imposed; and I hereby give you authority to execute them upon all those who fail to obey you.

Also, so that this my letter may be brought to the attention of all, and that none may plead ignorance of it, I command that it be read in the squares and markets and other customary places of the said Island of Española by the public crier, in the presence of a notary and witnesses, none of whom shall disobey it in any way, on pain of my displeasure and 50,000 *maravedís* for my treasury, to be levied against each offender. Moreover, I command him who shows them this my letter to cite them to appear before me at my court, wherever I may be, within one hundred days of the time they are cited, under the said penalty; and, also under the same penalty, I command any notary who should be called upon to do so, to give testimony thereof signed with his rubric, so that I may know how my command is being observed.

Done in this City of Burgos, December 27, 1512.

    I, the King
    I, Lope Conchillos, Secretary to the
      Queen our Mistress
    The Bishop of Palencia — Count
      [of Pernia]

AMENDMENTS TO THE LAWS OF BURGOS

Doña Juana, by the Grace of God Queen of Castile, León, Granada, Toledo, Galicia, Sevilla, Córdoba, Murcia, Jaén, the Algarbes, Algeciras, Gibraltar, the Canary Islands, and the Indies, Islands, and Mainland of the Ocean Sea; Princess of Aragón, the Two Sicilies, and Jerusalem; Archduchess of Austria; Duchess of Austria, Burgundy, and Brabant; Countess of Flanders and Tyrol; Lady of Biscay, Molina, etc.

To you, the Alcalde Mayor and constables of the Island of San Juan, which is in the Indies of the Ocean Sea, and to our officers of the said Island, and to all other justices and officers of it whatsoever, present and future, and to the town councils, justices, regidores, knights, squires, officers, and citizens of the said Island, its towns and villages, and to any other persons whatsoever to whom what is contained in this my letter may apply in any way, and to each and every one of you:

Know, that the King, my Lord and Father, and I, seeing how necessary it was for the service of God Our Lord, and ours, and for the salvation of souls and the increase and good treatment of the Indians of the said Island, as well as for its citizens, consulted prelates and religious and certain members of our Council, which we convened for the purpose, after which we commanded that certain ordinances be drawn up by which the said Indians were to be indoctrinated and taught and brought to a knowledge of our Holy Catholic Faith, and by which the said Indians were to be well treated and reduced to settlements, as is explained at greater length in the said ordinances. Thereupon the King, my Lord and Father, and I were informed that, although the said ordinances were very useful, profitable, and necessary, as well as fitting, it was said that some of them had need of further elucidation and modification. Therefore, since it has always been our intent, desire, and will, to have greater regard for the salvation of souls and the indoctrination and good treatment of the said Indians than for any other

consideration, we commanded several prelates and religious of the Order of St. Dominic, and several members of our Council, and preachers and learned men of good life and conscience, very prudent and zealous in the service of Our Lord, to consider the said ordinances and amend them, add to them or reduce them, and modify them as might be necessary. Therefore, having considered the said ordinances and listened to the religious who have knowledge of the affairs of the said Island and the conditions and habits of the said Indians, they, together with other prelates and members of our Council, amended and modified the said ordinances as follows.

I

First, we order and command that Indian women married to Indian men who have been given in encomienda shall not be forced to go and come and serve with their husbands, at the mines or elsewhere, unless it is by their own free will, or unless their husbands wish to take them; but the said wives shall be obliged to work on their own land or on that of their husbands, or on the lands of the Spaniards, who shall pay them the wages agreed upon with them or with their husbands; but if the said wives should be pregnant we command that the ordinances we issued covering this situation be observed, on pain that he who does the contrary shall, besides suffering the penalty prescribed in the said ordinance, lose the Indian woman whom he thus forces to work, as well as her husband and children, who shall be given in encomienda to others.

II

Also, we order and command that Indian children under fourteen years of age shall not be compelled to work at tasks [of adults] until they have attained the said age or more; but they shall be compelled to work at, and serve in, tasks proper to children, such as weeding the fields and the like, on their parents' estates (if they have parents); and those above the age of four-teen shall be under the authority of their parents until they are of age and married. Those who have neither father nor mother, we command shall be given in encomienda by the person who has our authority to do so, and he shall give them in charge to per-sons of good conscience who shall see that they are taught and indoctrinated in the things of our Holy Faith, and employ them on their estates in tasks set by our appellate judges, in which they can work without endangering their health, provided that they [the encomenderos] feed them and pay them their proper wages at the rate fixed by our said judges, and provided that they [the encomenderos] do not prevent their attendance at Christian doctrine at the appointed time. And if any of the said boys should wish to learn a trade they may freely do so, and they may not be compelled to serve in, or work at, anything else while they are learning the said trade.

III

Also, we order and command that un-married Indian women who are under the authority of their parents, mothers or fathers, shall work with them on their lands, or on the lands of others by agree-ment with their parents; and those not under the authority of their fathers and mothers shall, to prevent their becoming vagabonds and bad women, and to keep them from vice and teach them the doctine, be constrained to be with the other women and work on their estates, if they have such; otherwise, they shall work on the estates of the Indians and others, who shall pay them their wages at the rate they pay the others who work for them.

IV

Also, we order and command that within two years [of the publication of this ordi-nance] the men and women shall go about clad. And whereas it may so happen that in the course of time, what with their in-doctrination and association with Chris-tians, the Indians will become so apt and ready to become Christians, and so civilized and educated, that they will be capable of governing themselves and leading the kind of life that the said Christians lead there, we declare and command and say that it is our will that those Indians who thus be-come competent to live by themselves and govern themselves, under the direction and control of our said judges of the said Island, present or future, shall be allowed to live by themselves and shall be obliged to serve [only] in those things in which our vassals in Spain are accustomed to serve, so that they may serve and pay the tribute which they [our vassals] are accustomed to pay to their princes.

Therefore, I order and command that each and every one of you, the said Admiral, governor, judges, and officers, present or future, and any other persons whatsoever to whom the said ordinances apply or shall apply, to consider the first ordinances men-tioned [i.e., those of 1512], together with the amendments and modifications here in-corporated, to observe, obey, and execute them, in every way and by every means, as is prescribed in the said amendments and modifications; and while observing and obeying them yourselves, you shall execute and cause to be executed the penalties upon those who incur them; and you yourselves shall also obey them in the form and man-ner prescribed in the said ordinances. More-over, [in case of disobedience] you shall incur the penalty of the loss of the said property and be forbidden to hold the Indi-ans allotted to you in encomienda, as per-sons who have failed to indoctrinate or teach them or treat them with the charity with which they should be treated, and as it is our will that they be treated. Also, we avow that those of you who exceed what is here ordered shall be held accountable to God, and that this shall be a charge on your consciences. We say further that we do not give you faculty [to act otherwise], and that [in case of disobedience] you shall lose the Indians you have in encomienda and they shall be declared vacated, so that we may assign them to whomsoever we please; and you shall not act against the tenor and form of these ordinances, nor shall you consent to it at any time or in any way. And if [in order to execute them] you should have need of favor and aid, by this my letter I order all town councils, justices, regidores, alcaldes, and constables [of that Island] and of its towns and villages, and all our officers residing there, to render you such favor and aid as you may require in order to execute everything that is contained in this my letter and in each and every part of it.

And so that this my letter may come to the knowledge of all, I order that it and the ordinances contained therein be proclaimed by the public crier, in the squares, markets, and other customary places of the said Island, in the presence of a notary public and witnesses; and no one shall proceed against it in any way, on pain of my displeasure and a fine of 10,000 *maravedís*, to be paid into my treasury. Further, I order that those who disobey it shall be cited by him who shows them this my letter, to appear before me at my court, wherever I may be, within six months of the day when they are thus cited, under the same penalty. And under the same penalty I command any notary public whatsoever who is called upon for this purpose, to give him who shows him this my letter a certificate to that effect signed with his rubric, so that I may know how this my command is being observed.

Given in the City of Valladolid, July 28, 1513.

> *I, the King*
>
> *I, Lope Conchillos, Secretary to our Mistress the Queen, caused this to be inscribed, by order of the King her Father.*
>
> *Registered: Licenciatus Ximénez*
>
> *The Bishop of Palencia — Count [of Pernia]*
>
> *Castañeda, Chancellor*

CAMPAIGNING FOR THE INDIAN CAUSE

FRAY BARTOLOMÉ DE LAS CASAS

The most consistent, active, vociferous champion of the Indian cause on both sides of the Atlantic was the Dominican friar and later Bishop of Chiapas (Mexico), Fray Bartolomé de Las Casas (1474–1566). From conquistador and *encomendero* himself he became the severest critic of his former fellows. His writings are voluminous. Two short pieces have been assembled for inclusion herein. The first selection takes bits from the vigorous and sweeping condemnation of the Spaniards and their treatment of the Indians, *Brevísima relación de la destrucción de las Indias,* prepared in 1542 and presented to Prince Philip of Spain, but not published until 1552. The second selection is from his lengthy condemnation of the encomienda system, written about the same time and often referred to as *Octavo Remedio*—a key to the more pertinent of the twenty reasons adduced is given.

No attempt is made here to set down biographical data on Las Casas. His career is covered quite well in a number of the selections chosen for this volume. There are a number of editions of the *Brevísima Relación,* and several translations—the one here used is that of Francis Augustus MacNutt, with some emendations. The text of the *Octavo Remedio* can be found in *Colección de tratados, 1552–1553* (Buenos Aires: Instituto de investigaciones históricas, 1924), pp. 325–432.

From *Brevísima Relación*

PROLOGUE

As I have fifty, or more years of experience in those countries, I have therefore been considering the evil I have seen committed, the injuries, losses, and misfortunes, such as it would not have been thought could be done by man. . . . When some of their particular actions are made known to Your Highness [the piece is addressed to Prince Philip], it will not be possible to forbear supplicating His Majesty with importunate insistence, that he should not concede nor permit that which the tyrants have invented, pursued, and put into execution, calling it Conquests; which if per-

mitted, will be repeated; because these acts in themselves, done against those pacific, humble, and mild Indian people, who offend none, are iniquitous, tyrannous, condemned and cursed by every natural, divine, and human law. So as not to keep criminal silence concerning the ruin of numberless souls and bodies that these persons cause, I have decided to print some, though very few, of the innumerable instances I have collected in the past and can relate with truth, in order that Your Highness may read them with greater facility. . . . I therefore esteemed it right to furnish Your Highness with this very brief summary of a very long history that could and ought to be composed, of the massacres and devastation that have taken place. . . .

INTRODUCTION

Two ordinary and principal methods have the self-styled Christians, who have gone there, employed in extirpating these miserable nations and removing them from the face of the earth. The one, by unjust, cruel, and tyrannous wars. The other, by slaying all those who aspire to or sigh for or think of liberty or to escape from the torments that they suffer, such as all the native lords and adult men; for generally they leave none alive in the wars, except the young men and the women, whom they oppress with the hardest, most horrible, and roughest servitude, to which either man or beast can be put. . . . The reason why the Christians have killed and destroyed such infinite numbers of souls is solely because they have made gold their ultimate aim, seeking to load themselves with riches in the shortest time and to mount by high steps, disproportioned to their condition: namely by their insatiable avarice and ambition, the greatest that could be on earth. . . .

ESPAÑOLA

When the wars were finished, and with them the murder, they divided among them all the men (youths, women, and children being usually spared), giving to one thirty, to another forty, and to another a hundred and two hundred, according to the favor each enjoyed with the chief tyrant, whom they called governor. Having thus distributed them, they assigned them to each Christian, under the pretence that the latter should train them in the Catholic faith; thus to men who are generally all idiots, and very cruel, avaricious, and vicious, they gave the care of souls. The care and thought these Spaniards took was to send the men to the mines to dig gold, which is an intolerable labor; and they put the women into dwellings, which are huts, to dig and cultivate the lands, which is a strong and robust man's task. . . . It is impossible to recount the burdens with which their owners loaded them [the Indians], making them walk a hundred or more leagues with loads of seventy-five to a hundred pounds. The same Christians had themselves transported in net-like contraptions called *hamacas*. They thus used the Indians as beasts of burden. . . . To tell of the lashings, the beatings, the cuffs and blows and curses, and a thousand more kinds of torments to which their masters subjected them, while the Indians were, in truth, working hard, would take much time and more paper, and would be something to amaze mankind. . . .

CUBA

After all the Indians of this island were reduced to servitude and misfortune like those of Española, and when they saw that they were all perishing, many natives began to flee to the mountains, others to hang themselves in despair; husbands and wives hanged themselves together with their children. Through the cruelty of one very inhuman Spaniard, whom I knew, more than two hundred Indians did away with themselves. . . . There was an officer of the King in this island, to whose share three hundred Indians fell. By the end of three months he had, through labor in the mines, caused the death of two hundred and seventy, so that he had only thirty left, a tenth of his original grant. The authorities gave him as many again, and once more he killed them off. And they continued to supply Indians, and he to work them to death, until at last he died and the devil carried away his soul. . . .

NICARAGUA

The Spaniards kept within their own houses all the Indian lords, the aged, the women, and the youngsters, all of whom they compelled to serve them day and night, without rest. They used even the children as soon as they could stand and loaded them with tasks far beyond their capacity. . . . They have exhausted and oppressed and caused the premature death of many people in this Province, making them carry planks and timber to build vessels in the port; also by sending them to find honey and wax in the mountains, where they are devoured by tigers; and have loaded and still do load pregnant and confined women like animals. However, the most horrible practice, and the one which has helped most to destroy this Province, has been the license which the governor gave to the Spaniards to demand slaves from the princes and the lords of the Indian towns. Every four or five months or whenever one obtained the favor or license from the said governor, he asked the lord for fifty slaves, threatening, if he did not give them, to burn him alive or to deliver him to fierce dogs. As the Indians usually do not keep slaves, or at most a lord might have two or three, the lords went through their towns and took first of all the orphans; next, of those who had two children they asked one, and of those who had three, two. In this way the lord filled up the number demanded by the tyrant, amidst great wailing and weeping in the town, for they seem, more than any other people, to love their children. . . .

NEW SPAIN

Here it must be noted that the pretext with which they invaded and began to destroy all those innocent beings and to depopulate those lands which on account of their teeming populations should have caused such joy and satisfaction to true Christians, was that they came to subject them to the King of Spain. Otherwise, they must kill and make slaves of them. And those who did not promptly yield obedience to such an unreasonable and stupid command and who refused to put themselves in the hands of such iniquitous, cruel, and brutal men, they declared were rebels, who had risen against the service of His Majesty. . . . The blindness of those who govern the Indians kept them from understanding or observing what is expressed so clearly in their laws, namely, that no one can be called a rebel who is not first a subject. . . . Dreadful is it that those who obey volun-tarily are subjected to onerous servitude, in which under a regime of incredible labor and tortures they are worse off than those who died by the sword, and as a result they and their wives and their children and all their race perish. . . .

YUCATAN

This Tyrant [Francisco de Montejo], with three hundred men whom he had brought with him, began to make cruel war on those good and innocent people, who kept within their houses without offending anyone. They killed and destroyed countless people. The country produces no gold, and if it had he would have used up the people by working them in the mines. But, in order to coin gold out of the bodies and souls of those for whom Jesus Christ died, he made slaves of all whom he did not kill. Many ships were attracted thither by the news that slaves were to be had, and all of these he loaded and sent back with humans whom he sold for wine, oil, vinegar, pork, clothing, horses, and whatsoever else he and his men felt that they needed. . . .

SANTA MARTA

I truthfully declare that, if I had to relate singly the evil, the massacres, the destruction, injustice, violence, slaughter, and the great sins the Spaniards have committed in this Kingdom of Santa Marta, against God and King and these innocent nations, I would compose a very long history. All this I will relate in due time, if God gives me life. . . .

THE PEARL COAST

The tyranny exercised by the Spaniards upon the Indians in fishing pearls is as cruel and reprehensible a thing as there can be in the world. Upon the land there is no life so infernal and hopeless as to be compared to it, although that of digging gold in the mines is the hardest and worst. . . .

NEW GRANADA

And to prove the axiom I laid down in the beginning, namely, that the tyranny, violence, and injustice of the Spaniards towards these gentle lambs, accompanied by cruelty, inhumanity, and wickedness, most worthy of all fire and torture, which continue in the said provinces, go on increasing, I cite the following: After the massacres and slaughter of the war, the people are condemned, as was said, to the horrible slavery described above. To one of the devils, two hundred Indians were given, to another, three. The commandant ordered a hundred Indians to be called before him and, when they promptly came like so many lambs, he had the heads of thirty or forty cut off; and he said to the others: "I will do the same to you, if you do not serve me well or if you leave without my permission." Now in God's name consider, you who read this, what sort of deeds are these, and whether they do not surpass every imaginable cruelty and injustice, and whether it squares well with such Christians as these to call them devils; and whether it could be worse to give the Indians into the charge of the devils of hell than to the Christians of the Indies. . . .

I protest before God on my conscience that, as I believe and hold certain, such are the perdition, harm, destruction, depopulation, slaughter, death, and great and horrible cruelties, and most dastardly methods of violence, injustice, robbery, and massacre, done among these people and in all those countries of the Indies, that with all I have described, and those upon which I have expanded, I have not told nor enlarged upon, in quantity or quality, a ten thousandth part of what has been done and is being done today.

And that all Christians may have greater compassion on these innocent nations, and that they may more sincerely lament their loss and doom, and blame and abominate the detestable avarice, ambition, and cruelty of the Spaniards, let them all hold this truth for certain that, from the time the Indies were discovered down to the present, nowhere did the Indians harm any Christians, until they had sustained harm, robbery, and treachery from them. . . .

And something else might be added, namely, that from the beginning until the present day the Spaniards have given no more thought to providing for the preaching of the faith of Jesus Christ to these people than if they were dogs or other animals. Nay, they have consistently afflicted and persecuted the monks, to prevent them from preaching, because it seemed to the Spaniards that this might be an impediment to their acquisition of gold and wealth, such as they had promised themselves in their greedy desires. . . .

From *Octavo Remedio*

May Your Majesty order and command . . . that all the Indians throughout the Indies, both those today subject as well as those who in the future will be conquered, be put under the immediate jurisdiction of the Crown of Castile and Leon as subjects and free vassals; and that none be given in encomienda to the Christian Spaniards. . . . This is necessary for the twenty causes or reasons set down in the following:

First Reason: Because these kingdoms and the people thereof being infidels and in need of being converted to our holy faith have been committed and commended by God and the Apostolic See in His name to the Kings of Castile and Leon . . . these same lords, the Kings of Castile, cannot consider themselves freed of this task, care, and obligation by passing it on to another, since the thing is of such great importance. . . .

Second Reason: Since the reason for the grant of such jurisdiction to Your Majesty is that the faith may be preached and spread among these peoples and that they may be brought to a knowledge of Christ . . . Your Majesty is bound to eliminate any obstacles which might stand in the way of the achievement of this end. . . . One of the major obstacles has been that these Indians have been given in encomienda to the Christians. . . , who out of avarice and greed have prevented the religious from going into the Indian towns which they control. . . .

Third Reason: How many of the Spaniards who go to the Indies today are capable of giving the Indians whom they hold in encomienda instruction in the truths of our faith? . . .

Fifth Reason: It is according to reason that a privilege granted to a person should not be turned to the detriment of said person; therefore, the entire governance, rule, order, and manner of dealing with those Indians should be exclusively in the hands of Your Majesty, in such manner that they should receive nothing but good and profit, both spiritual and temporal, and both of these advantages Your Majesty alone can give. . . .

Sixth Reason: The Spaniards are manifestly the enemies and destroyers of the lives of these Indians. . . .

Seventh Reason: According to the laws of reason and justice, as all wise philosophers and moralists hold, never should jurisdiction be given to poor men, since these by ambition and greed will seek through inordinate means to rise above their poverty and to achieve riches and wealth and position. . . .

Eighth Reason: Having given the Indians in encomienda to the Spaniards, the poor natives are loaded and worn out by duties and services and other intolerable vexations. . . . They really have four lords: Your Majesty, their own caciques, the Spaniard to whom they have been commended, and the overseer whose yoke is very heavy and galling. . . .

Ninth Reason: These people, free by nature, should not lose that freedom by the fact that they accept Your Majesty as their lord. . . . It is evident that no power on earth can take away the fundamental freedom of free men. . . .

Tenth Reason: It is a just thing and the law of reason which decrees that one who has used a privilege badly ought to be deprived of the same. . . . [The encomenderos have so done; therefore. . . .]

Twelfth Reason: If Your Majesty does not remove the Indians from the control of the Spaniards, there soon will be no Indians. . . .

Thirteenth Reason: Giving the Indians to the Spaniards in what manner soever is highly prejudicial to the Crown and to Spain. . . . Your Majesty is losing a vast number of vassals who are being destroyed by the cruelty of the Spaniards . . . the Crown is losing much treasure . . . the Church is losing the souls of both Indians and Spaniards, the latter seemingly are in league with the devil himself. . . .

Seventeenth Reason: Were Your Majesty to withdraw the Indians from under the power of the Spanish encomenderos and take them all directly under the jurisdiction of the Crown, there is nothing which would give greater joy to the Indians or win greater loyalty for the Crown on their part. . . .

Twentieth Reason: The Twentieth and last reason which we give is this: by eliminating the encomiendas Your Majesty would bestow on all Spaniards, in the Indies and in all of the Spanish Empire, an inestimable blessing: You would be preserving them from the grave sins of tyranny, robbery, violence, murder, which they daily commit through their oppression of these peoples. . . .

These twenty reasons which we have here set down, in order that this cruel tyranny may be brought to an end, which is so destructive of so considerable a portion of the human race, which has devastated and exterminated the Indies, and could well have depopulated the rest of the world, if for forty-five years in other parts of the world, as here, it had been practised; these twenty reasons, to repeat, we affirm before God and our conscience, and these we believe, on the basis of our long experience, and we hold that they, singly and together, are sufficient reason why Your Majesty should neither desire nor ought to, nor can concede these repartimientos of Indians to ambitious, greedy, and insensitive men, who with so much insistence demand them, for such men destroy the honor and glory of God; they render our faith infamous and odious; they depopulate the world of so many peoples, sending these benighted folk to hell who die without the faith and without the Sacraments.

The grave harm which has come to the royal crown of Castile and Leon because of these acts and which will come to the whole of Spain, the blind will see, the deaf will hear, the dumb will proclaim, and thoughtful men will censure. . . .

ANSWER TO LAS CASAS

ANTONIO DE LEÓN PINELO

Antonio Rodríguez de León Pinelo (d.1660) was born in Peru toward the end of the sixteenth century. He early became interested in the history of the New World and, not finding sufficient research material on the colonial side of the Atlantic, gravitated toward the mother country, where he spent much of his life. He served as *oidor* for the *Contratación de Cádiz* and later as *relator* in the Council of the Indies. He is properly credited as having through his immense bibliographical labors laid much of the groundwork for the future *Recopilación de leyes de los reynos de las Indias,* published in 1681. He is said to have worked through some 400,000 royal decrees and arrived at a condensation which itself bulked to 11,000 laws. This selection from his *Tratado* has been chosen as an example of an answer to some of the charges of Las Casas, especially those detailed in his *Treinta proposiciones* and his *Octavo remedio.*

HAVING answered in general terms the difficulty proposed, it remains to reply, in particular, to the objections which can be adduced and which the Bishop of Chiapa [Las Casas] actually has made, since in doing so the problem will become clearer. These objections of the bishop are twenty in number, although not all of them have the same force.

The first is that, since the Indies and their inhabitants have been entrusted by the Apostolic See to the kings of Castile, so truly Catholic, in order that through their conscientious care the natives may be brought to a knowledge of the true God, and since this is a personal commission and envisions the immediate governance and special attention which they should exercise over the said people, no person other than the King of Castile can be equal to this task. It follows that the monarchs cannot entrust this duty and care to another, yielding high or low jurisdiction over these nations, nor can they delegate to another nor commend these natives to another, even though the monarchs retain the universal and supreme overlordship.

To this objection the answer is made that this obligation to govern and convert the Indies was not given with the idea that the

From Antonio de León Pinelo, *Tratado de confirmaciones reales de encomiendas, oficios i casos, en que se requieren para las Indias occidentales* (Madrid, 1630), pp. 99–103.

kings personally perform these duties, but that they provide for the principal end, namely, that of promulgating the faith of Jesus Christ, through their ministers, just as they rule their other kingdoms, and by such laws and orders as they will deem proper and necessary. It is impossible to do the one without the other, even as the Bishop of Chiapa states in another place. This governance and care is not impeded, suspended, or blocked by the encomiendas, as they are today in practice, according to which the king gives no jurisdiction nor dominion over the Indians; nor is there any diminution of the royal prerogative in the matter of government, since it remains intact and lodged in the royal ministers and councils, without the encomenderos, who do not enjoy the right of personal service from the Indians, being able to ordain, or command, or operate in any area pertaining to the natives. And so the officers of the crown, and the right which these have to defend the crown's prerogatives in the matter, are charged with the care of the Indians, and further the special protectors who have been created for this purpose; the chancelleries and viceroys and the Council have been entrusted in a special manner with the supervision and good treatment of the Indians.

It is not contrary to all this to grant the Indians in encomienda to Spaniards, with the monarchs ceding to the Spaniards the tribute which rightfully belongs to the crown — even the Bishop concedes this last point. This transfer of tribute is one of interests, benefits, and utility only, and has nothing to do with the encomenderos' power of dominion, jurisdiction, or with any basic right to demand such tribute; this right remains always with the king and his ministers. From this, then, without going counter to the main goal, the conversion of the natives, flows a temporal good, namely, the preservation, peopling, and protection of those lands and the governance and education of the Indians; thus the Catholic faith is more fully served.

There are three classes of gentiles in these our times who are to be found in the Indies of the East and of the West. There is the first class, of good intelligence, tractable character, and highly civilized, who seem to lack nothing other than the faith of Christ. Such are the Chinese and the Japanese and other nations of the Orient, as is evident from the reports about them. In the second category are those who have states with kings and monarchs, but who enjoy only weak government not always capable of enforcing the natural precepts, and who are not as docile, firm, and constant; among these, along with some good laws, exist much barbarism. The third group is barbarous, uncivilized, and uneducated, who live like brute animals, without laws, king, or government. In the second class may be ranged the peoples of Peru and of Mexico, who live under a regime of law and government. The natives of Brazil, the Caribs, the Indians of Chile, the Chiriguanes, the Chichimecos, and the folk of the Marañón, should be ranged in the third class.

Each of these three classes requires its own special method of control and of evangelization. It is enough in the case of the first class that the faith be preached to them by the methods commonly used by the apostles of Christianity. Once they have embraced the faith, they will know how to preserve it and to defend it, as is amply proved by the martyrs in China and Japan. And though it is harder to establish the faith among such peoples, once done, the faith is firmly grounded and does not require the protection of a foreign government.

In the second class, less gifted and less mentally resistant, the faith is introduced with greater ease but it is less well understood and is not nearly so firmly grounded. Here too the faith alone should be preached, but, once accepted, there is need for a temporal prince who will govern and maintain and protect it; because left to themselves these new converts often fail to live up to what they profess and as often blaspheme by their actions the holy law of God. Therefore, they should be put under a regime which, founded on Christian principles, will help them to live peaceably and to replace their unholy customs with those which are just, honest, and reasonable.

Those in the third category, since they are brutish and uncivilized, must first be educated in matters which pertain to this life, before they can be trained in those of heaven. It is unlikely that they who do not know the things basically human and terrestrial will excel in their understanding of things divine and celestial. Hence, first must come a temporal and political government, as a necessary prerequisite; later can come the spiritual and ecclesiastical regime. This is amply proved in the memorials of Padre Fray Juan de Silva, which the Council of the Indies has ordered to be published; the same is also proved in the writings of Doctor Juan de Solorzano Pereyra, even though in his works he was treating of a quite other matter.

From this it follows that, since the Indians of the West are not like those of the first class but fall into the second and the third classes, they need the governance, protection, and supervision of the kings of Castile, to whom the Holy See has entrusted their instruction, conversion, and protection. This trust cannot be fulfilled without the ministers and tribunals who govern and defend them; the Indians are incapable of doing these things, if the Spaniards are not among them. Hence, these temporal goals must be first achieved, if conversion is to be made possible.

Were one to maintain that the Apostles preached to all peoples in one and the same manner and that thus our distinction is not valid and that it is enough for any nation to hear the word of God in order to accept and cherish it, then we might reply with another argument. When the faith was preached by the Apostles, they confirmed their words with miracles. Even though they preached in Europe, in Asia, in Africa, and as some people hold also in our Indies, places in which were to be found folk from all the three classes described above, the only nations in which the faith endured were those in which there was strong government. . . . How many of the nations of Asia and Africa have lost the faith precisely because of their barbarism and lack of strong government? With such examples before us, should we not in the case of our Indies take the proper measures to avoid like consequences?

We have seen the need for maintaining the government of Spain in the Indies, without which the faith cannot be preserved. Now, such government cannot endure without some reward to the men who by their glorious deeds made Spanish dominion possible. But there seems to be no other way of achieving this end than by distributing encomiendas. Hence, such grants appear to be justified. Without these rewards there would be no evangelization, no preservation of the faith implanted, no new discoveries, and the lands won might well be lost; with no hope of reward the soldiers and settlers would hardly be inspired to undertake such labors.

The Bishop of Chiapa posed this question and sought to solve it in two ways. First: he contends that, if the kings were to be without all these possessions overseas and if the Indians were never to be Christians, unless they were killed off and annihilated, the first alternative would be preferable to the second. Second: without the encomiendas the Indians would survive and there would actually be more Spaniards in the Indies. How this might happen we cannot say, for the bishop is supposed to have given the solution in a memorial which was never printed and, therefore, is not available to us. But if we take the first point and study it carefully, we must deny that the encomiendas are the cause of the extinction and annihilation of the Indians. Thus, we must conclude that the encomenderos have their grants legitimately and that the king has the full right to make such three ways. The first is the statement that the encomenderos do not allow religious to grants as a reward for services rendered, provided he retains for the Royal Crown, as he has done, the ports and capitals of those provinces, because of their importance for the defense and security of the kingdom. With this the first of the Bishop's arguments is refuted.

The Bishop's second objection is based on the first, namely, that it is the obligation of the kings of Castile to provide for the conversion of the Indians, because it is under this title that they have the right to the Indies. He argues: The monarchs must remove everything which can prove an obstacle or a hindrance to this end; the encomiendas are such an obstacle; therefore, they must be prohibited. He seeks to prove the minor proposition in this syllogism in come into their towns to preach the Gospel. . . . The second is that sometimes a town is given to three or four encomenderos, who thus divide the Indians among themselves, one taking the parents, another the sons, a third the relatives, and thus the Indians are separated and dispersed and deprived of their freedom, whereas being together as families and free is more conducive to their conversion. The third is that the encomenderos have very little care in seeing that their Indians are instructed in the faith.

We answer this objection by conceding the major but denying the minor and the three reasons given to support it. . . . [*The jousting goes on through the score of objections offered by Las Casas — this short excerpt may give the reader some idea of the type and manner of argumentation used by the author.*]

THE TEN PLAGUES OF NEW SPAIN

MOTOLINÍA

Motolinía (Fray Toribio de Paredes de Benavente) was one of the Franciscan "Twelve Apostles" who came to New Spain in 1524. We know that he was born in Benavente, but the year is uncertain; he died in Mexico, presumably, in 1565, after forty very full years of apostolic labors among the Indians of New Spain.

Motolinía is often noted as one of the bitterest and most outspoken critics of Las Casas—his *Carta al Emperador Carlos V* of January 2, 1555, does indeed lash out strongly against the Dominican, but it is opposed not to his aims but to some of his methods and much of the exaggeration found in his writings. Motolinía, quite as readily as Las Casas, condemned the Spaniards for their cruelties and abuses. The following selection will so demonstrate. But Fray Toribio, as he himself asserts in his *Historia*, "made every effort not to offend against the truth in what I am saying."

GOD struck and chastised this land and those who were in it, natives as well as foreigners, with ten disastrous plagues.

The first plague was an epidemic of smallpox. . . .

The second plague was the great number of deaths that occurred during the conquest of New Spain, and especially of Mexico [that is Mexico City]. . . .

From *Motolinía's History of the Indians of New Spain*, translated and annotated, with a bio-bibliographical study of the author, by Francis Borgia Steck, O.F.M. (Washington: Academy of American Franciscan History, 1951), pp. 87–93. Reprinted by permission of the Academy of American Franciscan History.

The third plague was dire famine that followed after the city of Mexico was taken.

The fourth plague was the *calpixques* or overseers, and the Negroes. When the land was apportioned, the conquerors placed in the *repartimientos* and towns that were granted them in *encomienda*, servants or Negroes who were to collect the tributes and look after the granaries. The *calpixques* would live, and they still live, in the towns. Even though they are for the most part farmers from Spain, they have become overlords in this land and command its principal native chiefs as if these were their slaves. Because I have no desire to lay bare their shortcomings, I shall pass over in silence what I think, merely saying that they make the natives serve and fear them as if they themselves were absolute and native lords. They do nothing but make demands and, no matter how much is done for them, they are not satisfied. Wherever they are, they spoil and corrupt everything, emitting a stench like spoiled meat. They make no effort to do anything but to command. They are the drones that consume the honey which is worked by the poor bees, the Indians. What the poor people are able to give them does not satisfy them. They are unreasonable. . . .

The fifth plague was the heavy tribute and services which the Indians rendered. Since the Indians kept in the temples of the idols, in the trust of their lords and chiefs, and in numerous sepulchers, a great quantity of gold which they had collected over a period of many years, the Spaniards began to extract heavy tributes from these sources. Because of the fear which the Indians entertained of the Spaniards ever since the war, they surrendered all that they possessed. But the tributes were so continuous that scarcely had they paid one when they were obliged to pay another. In order to be able to meet their obligations, the Indians would sell their children and their lands to the merchants. Failing to meet their obligation, very many died in consequence, some from torture and others from cruel imprisonment, since they were treated inhumanly and regarded as being lower than beasts.

The sixth plague was the gold mines. In addition to the tributes and services which the people rendered, the Spaniards soon began to look for mines. The Indian slaves who up to the present have died in these mines cannot be counted. Gold, in this land, was adored as a god in the form of a calf. People came from Castile to adore it, undergoing innumerable hardships and dangers. What they have already acquired, may it please the Lord that it be not unto their damnation.

The seventh plague was the building of the great city of Mexico. . . .

The eighth plague was the slave labor employed in working the mines. So great was the haste with which in some years slaves were made that from all parts there entered Mexico great flocks of them, like sheep, so that they could be easily branded. Those who were called slaves in the sense of the Indians were not sufficient in number. Even if some were slaves according to the cruel and barbarous law of the Indians, the fact is that only a few were legally and actually slaves. On account of the haste with which the Indians were made to bring such a large number of slaves every eighty days as tribute, many of these slaves died. Accordingly, when the number of available slaves was exhausted they brought their children and the *macehuales*, who were of a lower caste and were similar to vassal laborers, and of these they brought as many more as they could find and assemble; whereupon they intimidated them to such an extent that they would admit that they were slaves. Since the investigation was not made with much care and the branding iron was ready at hand, slaves were branded so often that, in addition to the principal royal brand, their whole face was marked up, because as often as a slave was bought and sold he was branded. For this reason the eighth plague is not to be considered the least disastrous.

The ninth plague was the provisioning of the mines. To these mines Indian carriers would travel seventy leagues and more in order to bring sustenance. The food which they carried for their own use sometimes gave out, either on the way to the mines or on the return trip before they reached home. Some carriers the miners detained for some days in order that they might help extract the mineral, while others would be employed in building houses or in rendering personal service. During this time food would give out and the Indians would die either there in the mines or on the road, since they had no money with which to buy food and there was no one to give it to them. Other carriers returned home in such a condition that they soon died. . . .

The tenth plague was the dissensions and factions among the Spaniards living in Mexico. . . .

ON THE NEW LAWS

LESLEY BYRD SIMPSON

Rather than bore the reader with large and long quotations from contemporary documents, not always too interesting in their original form, this and the next two selections give two important sources in summary fashion—and often with valuable historical background and commentary. Simpson and Hanke review the famous New Laws of 1542. These New Laws mark an attempt, unsuccessful in the long run, on the part of the Crown to eliminate that institution of the *encomienda* which had drawn such severe criticism from Las Casas and other champions of the Indians and had been considered by them as the real root of the evils which had grown up in the Indian-Spaniard relationship.

THE encomenderos of the time, as well as Motolinía, saw in Las Casas the cause of all their woes. Whatever his contribution to the New Laws was, the thesis upon which they were based was the ancient one of the Dominicans which was used in the Laws of Burgos. Its best expression was voiced by Francisco de Vitoria in his two lectures, *De Indis recenter inventis* and *De jure belli Hispanorum in barbaros,* delivered at the University of Salamanca in 1532. Vitoria's conclusions struck at the very foundation of Spanish temporal power in the New World. They are, in brief:

1. Since unbelief does not preclude ownership of property, the Indians are not precluded from owning property, and they are therefore the true owners of the New World, as they were before the advent of the Spaniards.

2. The Emperor is not the lord of the whole world, and, even if he were, he would not therefore be entitled to seize the provinces of the Indians, to put down their lords, to raise up new ones, and to levy taxes.

3. Neither is the Pope the civil or temporal lord of the whole world. He has no secular power except in so far as it subserves things spiritual. He can have no power over the dominions of unbelievers and therefore cannot give such dominions to secular princes. A refusal on the part of the aborigines to recognize the power of the Pope cannot therefore be regarded as a reason for making war upon them and seizing their goods. If the Christian reli-

From Lesley Byrd Simpson, *The Encomienda in New Spain* (Berkeley, 1950), pp. 127–144. Reprinted by permission of the University of California Press.

gion had been expounded to the Indians with ever so much sufficiency of proof, and they still refused to accept it, this would not render it lawful to make war upon them and despoil them of their possessions.

4. The Spaniards, on the other hand, have the right to go to the lands of the Indians, dwell there and carry on trade, so long as they do no harm, and they may not be prevented by the Indians from so doing. If the Spaniards have diligently informed the Indians that they have not come to interfere in any way with the peace and welfare of the Indians, and if the Indians still show hostility toward them and attempt to destroy them, then, and only then, will it be lawful to make war upon the Indians. In the event of war the Indians may be despoiled of their goods and reduced to slavery, because in the law of nations whatever we take from the enemy becomes ours at once, and so true is this that men may be brought into slavery to us.

5. The Christians have the right to preach the Gospel among the barbarians. The Pope has the right to entrust the conversion of the Indians to the Spaniards alone and to forbid all other nations to preach or trade among them, if the propagation of the Faith would thus be furthered. If the Indians do not hinder the preaching of the Gospel they may not be subjected by war, whether they accept it or not.

In spite of the uncomfortable implications of Vitoria's thesis, the Crown found it very useful in its attack upon the encomienda. Las Casas elaborated it in his "Eighth Remedy for the Ills of the Indies" which he presented at Valladolid before a special council summoned by Charles V to draw up a new Indian code. It is unnecessary to repeat Las Casas' argument, which had not changed essentially since the time of the Laws of Burgos. His conclusion will explain two things: (1) his usefulness to the Crown, and (2) why he aroused such bitter resentment in the Indies. "Let your Majesty," he said, "order and command . . . that all the Indians in all the Indies, those who have been subjected as well as those who may be subjected, be placed and reduced and incorporated in the Royal Crown of Castile and León . . . as the subjects and

vassals which they are, and let none be given in encomienda to any Christian Spaniard. Rather, let it be an inviolable royal constitution, determination, and law perpetually that neither now nor at any time may they ever be taken or alienated from the said Royal Crown, or given to anyone as vassals, or in encomienda, or in deposit, or by any other title, mode or manner of alienation, or taken from the Royal Crown because of services rendered by anyone, or because of any merit he may have or need he may suffer, for any cause or pretext whatever." In short, let there be one encomendero, the King. It is probable that Charles V was moved to take this grave decision by the current anarchy in Peru, where the squabble between Pizarro and Almagro had begun the long series of civil wars which all but destroyed that rich kingdom. However it was, it is here submitted that only such a consideration could have induced the sagacious Charles to approve the dangerous innovations of the New Laws. It may be allowed that he was not unaffected by the pious arguments of Las Casas; but he was first of all a Hapsburg despot engaged in consolidating his vast empire, and he could not consistently have tolerated feudalism in the Indies. He was also perennially in need of funds, and the seizure of the wealth of the encomenderos must be reckoned among his motives.

The gravity of the issues and the lengthy debates of the council of Valladolid prevented an early decision; in consequence it was reconstituted and reconvened at Barcelona. The influence of Dominican thought on its conclusions is at once apparent. Of the fifty-four articles of the New Laws, twenty-three concerned the status and treatment of the Indians, and all but a few of the most radical were eventually incorporated into the *Recopilación*. The twenty-three are summarized below.

Art. 10 The Indians are free persons and vassals of the Crown, and it has always been the royal purpose to have them treated as such. The Council of the Indies is therefore commanded to see to the execution of the laws for their benefit and protection.

Art. 24. It is one of the principal duties of the audiencias to enquire into and punish excesses committed against the Indians.

Art. 25. Lawsuits among the Indians are to be decided summarily and according to their usage and custom.

Art. 26. We order and command that henceforth, for no reason of war or any other, even though it be by reason of rebellion or purchase, may any Indian be made a slave, and we wish them to be treated as our vassals of the Crown of Castile, which they are. No person may make use of any Indian, either as naboria or tapia, or in any other way, against his will.

Art. 27. Since we have ordered that henceforth in no wise shall Indians be made slaves . . . we order and command that the audiencias, having summoned both parties, shall summarily and briefly, without quibbling, the truth only having been ascertained, set them at liberty, if the persons who hold them as slaves do not show title of legitimate possession; and in order that, because of failure to petition . . . the Indians do not remain slaves, we order the audiencias to place persons to plead these suits for the Indians, and let them be paid out of the court fines, and let them be men of confidence and diligence.

Art. 28. The use of Indian carriers is to be permitted only in those places where it cannot be avoided, and then only with their consent, moderately, and for pay.

Art. 30. No free Indian is to be brought to the pearl fisheries against his will; if the loss of life in pearl-diving cannot be avoided, pearl-fishing is to be abandoned.

Art. 31. All Indians held in encomienda by the viceroys, by their lieutenants, royal officers, prelates, monasteries, hospitals, religious houses, mints, the treasury, etc., are to be transferred forthwith to the Crown.

Art. 32. Excessively large encomiendas are to be reduced in size and the surplus of Indians is to be distributed among those first conquerors who have none.

Art. 33. Those encomenderos who have mistreated their Indians are to lose their encomiendas, which will be placed in the Crown.

Art. 35. *Also we order and command that henceforth no viceroy, governor, audiencia, discoverer, or other person, may give Indians in encomienda by our provision, or by renun-* *ciation, donation, sale, or in any other form or means . . . but upon the death of the person holding the said Indians, let them be placed in our royal Crown;* and the audiencias have the duty of informing [us] immediately of the person who died, his quality, merits, and services, and how he treated his Indians, and whether he left a widow, children, or other heirs; and let them send us an account of the quality of the Indians and the land, so that we may provide what is best for our service and make a grant, according to our pleasure, to the widow and children of the deceased; and if meanwhile it is the opinion of the audiencia that the widow and children should be given some support, let them do so with the tributes paid by the Indians [of the deceased's encomienda], giving them a moderate sum, but leaving the Indians in our Crown, as has been said.

Art. 36. The Indians removed from the encomiendas are to be well treated and taught in the Holy Catholic Faith as free vassals of the Crown, and that is to be the principal concern of the presidents and oidores of the audiencias. These Indians are to be governed in the manner now prevailing in New Spain for the Crown Indians [i.e., in corregimientos].

Art. 37. In the distribution of corregimientos the first conquerors are to be preferred.

Art. 38. Lawsuits involving Indians are no longer to be tried in the Indies, or by the Council of the Indies, but must be pleaded before the King himself.

Art. 39. In expeditions of discovery no Indians are to be used, save only perhaps three or four as interpreters. One or two religious are to accompany each expedition. Nothing may be taken from the Indians except in fair trade.

Art. 42. The tributes of newly discovered Indians are to be fairly assessed and delivered to the royal treasurer.

Art. 43. The Spaniards have no authority whatever over newly discovered Indians and may not use them in any way whatever. They may have the use of only such tributes as the governor shall approve.

Art. 45. The Indians left alive in the islands of Puerto Rico, Cuba, and Española are relieved of all tributes and services, so that they may multiply and be taught in the Holy Catholic Faith.

Art. 46. Those first conquerors and their heirs who have no Indians in encomienda are to be provided for out of the tributes of the

Indians removed from encomiendas.

Art. 47. Corregimientos are to be assigned preferably to those conquerors who were not provided for [in the distribution of encomiendas], and to their sons.

Art. 48. Encomenderos must reside in the provinces in which their encomiendas are located.

Art. 49. The tributes paid to encomenderos and to the Crown are to be fixed at a lower rate than that which obtained under the native rulers.

Art. 50. The Indians are to be well treated as free vassals of the Crown, which they are. Anyone mistreating them is to be punished according to the laws of Castile.

Art. 51. No encomendero may exact a greater tribute from his Indians than that fixed by the viceroy and the Audiencia.

Although there was very little in the New Laws that had not been projected or enacted already, it was evident to the colonists that this time the Crown meant them to stick. Many of the "first conquerors" had already died, and their encomiendas were held by their widows and heirs. Many others were aging and faced the prospect of leaving their dependents with nothing but a vaguely promised pension. The encomenderos also, with some justice, it must be admitted, looked upon themselves as a vested aristocracy, but for whom there would have been no New World for the Spanish Crown to enjoy. The progress of the councils of Valladolid and Barcelona was anxiously watched from every corner of the Indies, and the publication of the New Laws was awaited with sullen resentment. Cortés, who had his ear to the ground along with the rest of the worried encomenderos, wrote to the Council of the Indies what was to become a standard form letter in support of the encomienda. After reminding the Council that the encomenderos were the only military force in New Spain, he hinted darkly at "the indignation it would cause to remove them [the Indians], not only among those who have them, but among those who are supported by them [i.e., the clergy]." The removal of the encomienda

would destroy commerce and, with it, his Majesty's revenue. Anyway, whatever harm the Indians suffered from the encomienda could be avoided by giving them "to the proper people," who would conserve them, "and his Majesty's rents would increase and become permanent."

The Crown did not entrust the execution of these unpopular laws to the existing authorities in New Spain and Peru, where opposition was the strongest. Four men were commissioned to enforce them: Blasco Núñez Vela, for Peru; Francisco Tello de Sandoval, for New Spain; Miguel Díaz de Armendáriz, for Tierra Firme; and Alonso López de Cerrato, for the Antilles and the Pearl Coast. Blasco Núñez Vela was unlucky enough to arrive in Peru during the rebellion of Gonzalo Pizarro, and was promptly captured and beheaded. It is not unreasonable to assume that New Spain would also have suffered the horrors of a civil war if Antonio de Mendoza and Juan de Zumárraga had not been able to persuade Tello de Sandoval to suspend the laws affecting the encomienda until an appeal could be presented to the Council of the Indies.

The articles of the New Laws which most profoundly affected the administration and economic life of the colony were numbers 26 and 27, abolishing Indian slavery; 31, prohibiting the holding of encomiendas by public servants and institutions, by the secular clergy and religious establishments; and 35, forbidding new encomiendas and providing that encomiendas escheat to the Crown upon the death of their present holders. This last was the one which aroused the fiercest opposition and which the Crown was soon forced to abrogate.

In New Spain there was an unexpected unanimity of opinion opposed to the abolition of the encomienda. Tello de Sandoval circulated the inevitable interrogatory, in order, we may safely conjecture, to cover himself at Court. It contained three questions: (1) Is it necessary for the service of God and his Majesty to have the Indians held in encomienda? (2) Should the new law concerning this matter be set aside? (3) If many Indians should be left idle because they were not held in encomienda, what difficulties would arise?

Of all the replies received that of the Dominican chapter at Mexico City is easily the most significant, because it was that order which had most violently opposed the encomienda from the beginning. One of its signers was Domingo de Betanzos, old friend and supporter of Las Casas, and the one who had induced him to join the order in 1522. To the first question they replied that it was necessary for the Indians to be held in encomienda, because it was apparent to all men that the Indians were so fickle by nature that they would never of themselves retain the religion they had received. There could be no permanence in the land without rich men, and there could be no rich men without encomiendas, because all industry was carried on with Indian labor, and only those with Indians could engage in commerce. Moreover, it was necessary to have rich men for defense against enemies and for protection of the poor, as was true in Spain and in every other well-regulated republic. Also, if there were rich men in the country with a permanent title to their estates trade would increase, and with it his Majesty's revenues.

The Indians [they wrote], receive great benefits from having the Spaniards hold their towns, for the Spaniards treat them as if they were their own children and the inheritance which their children are to receive. For this reason they try to conserve them and govern them, and to foment Christianity and bring religious to their towns. It may be allowed that there has been some negligence in the matter, but no one now desires anything but the good treatment of the Indians because of the justice and order which the viceroy has established, and because of the affection which the Spaniards now have for their Indians, as well as their own interest, for they know that their wealth depends upon the prosperity of their towns. And if the Indians cannot pay their tributes on time we know that their encomenderos will not press them, and that

they frequently forgive them [the payment]. Such is not the case with the towns held in corregimiento, for the Indians there are commonly thrown into jail on this account. Allowing that there are some good corregidores, yet it commonly happens that all they do is to collect their salaries and the tributes, and no good comes to the towns, but rather vexations and violence, as everyone knows. And, since the corregidores are poor and are so frequently changed, the saying is true that they do nothing but skin the Indians.

The encomenderos were necessary for the defense of the country, because they maintained and supported men in their encomiendas and fitted them out every year. Without the encomenderos to protect them, what would become of the poorer Spaniards? In that event the poor could not live in the country, unless they should become servants of the Indians, "which would be a great insult to the Christians and to the Spanish nation."

If the law should not be repealed it was certain that most of the people and the best people would leave the country rather than abandon their wives and children to the Indians. The estates of the encomenderos had become worthless and without price since the publication of the new law, and many of the married men were leaving the country, despairing of being confirmed in their encomiendas. If confirmation should not be received soon all would leave who could find buyers for their property, "and it is a most true fact that if they leave, your Majesty will not in a long time be able to reëstablish this country with people as noble and as attached to the soil as they are."

To the second question the Dominicans replied that the new law revoking the encomiendas might have been fitting and even necessary in certain other parts of the Indies, but not in New Spain, where the abuses of the Indians had ceased and the Indians were generally well treated. They also thought that since his Majesty had made the grants of the encomiendas after such abuses had ceased and the encomenderos had married and had many children, it was not just that these grants should be revoked without any present blame on their part. Rather, since they had won the country for his Majesty at their own expense and with great hardship and peril, it was just that his Majesty should renew the grants and make them perpetual, because otherwise the discontent and troubles of the present time would be repeated.

To the third question they made the hallowed *pro forma* reply: "As everyone knows, the Indians are weak by nature and are satisfied with having enough to get along on from day to day. And if there is any way to bring them out of their laziness and carelessness, it is to make them help the Spaniards in their commerce. In it the Indians are benefited through their wages, and thus they will become fond of commerce and profits, as, indeed, some of them have already done, in imitation of the Spaniards. . . . And, besides this, great good comes to the state and to his Majesty from having the Indians help the Spaniards in their commerce and on their estates, because without Indians all trade and profit cease. . . ."

It would not be difficult to pick flaws in the logic of the Dominican friars, or, at least, to challenge their assumptions; but we must consider them in their time. They accepted an Aristotelian world of masters and servants; they belonged to the master class and recognized their responsibilities. We cannot believe that they would have composed such a document from motives of worldly interest alone. The saintly life of Domingo de Betanzos and his companions is proof to the contrary. It must be concluded that they had come to accept the encomienda, as the Franciscans had long since done, as the best means of Christianizing the Indians and of bringing them to a proper (European) way of life. In a word, they had accepted the colonial attitude toward the Indians.

The Bishop of Oaxaca, Juan de Zárate, wrote a gossipy letter to Prince Philip which reveals not only his attitude toward the encomenderos and the New Laws, but also sheds some light on conditions in that stronghold of Cortés.

Temporal affairs in this city of Antequera are completely ruined . . . because, since the estate of the Marqués del Valle has not been defined and since Oaxaca (which is the same thing as Antequera) is his, the viceroy has not come to see it or visit it, and the citizens of the said Antequera suffer great necessities, hardships, and difficulties, because there are few who are rich, and if there ever were any [rich] they are dead. . . . The city [of Antequera] is abandoned and without people and in great danger, because there is not a fort or any defense whatever, and the natives have not given up their thought of rebellion, as there [in Spain] it is alleged. . . . In short, one cannot help regretting that . . . the city of Antequera of your Highness and the Oaxaca of the Marqués are held by two different lords — which is good neither for the Spaniards nor the natives, because the Spaniards have no place to sow or reap except in the lands of the natives; nor does the city have a common, or approaches, or pastures of its own. For this reason the natives cannot be as well treated as they should, because [the Spaniards] cannot avoid doing them harm with their cattle. . . . For the same reason there is no wheat in the city except that of the Marqués; nor are there any provisions except those brought in by his Indians, and all at such excessive prices that no one can support himself there. . . . The city is almost abandoned by the Spaniards, so much so that there are not above thirty citizens left, and they are looking for some way to leave, as they will, and it will be a desert (I mean without Spaniards) unless the matter is soon remedied by [your] ordering all those who have Indians to remain in the city and [by ordering] corregimientos given to those who live there . . . so that as a city, and one of the most important in this country, it may have a common and a pasture, and its citizens lands on which to sow and to plant trees, because for our sins vines do not yield there, although they have been planted, with no little expense and hardship, and with too many conflicts with the natives and with the servants of the Marqués. . . . The natives have increased and have intruded into the outlying parts of the said city, not leaving the Spaniards any egress for their cattle, or any common or pasture land for their cattle, or lands to work and cultivate.

The corregimientos, according to Bishop Zárate, were in very bad shape. The corregidores had to travel as far as a hundred leagues to Mexico City to collect their salaries and deliver their tributes. Not a few of them had to spend their entire salaries in the collection of tributes and in the government of the corregimientos. If they did not bring their tributes to Mexico City they destroyed them and, in order not to have to account for them, they jailed the Indians (to prevent the news from getting out), so that they might receive their appointments for the coming year.

Not so with the encomenderos, "who, by giving [the Indians] terms [in the payment of their tributes] and by teaching them the commerce of Castile and helping them over hard times, collect their tributes and make a living. Thus one small town [in encomienda] supports a Spaniard very well, while four towns [in corregimiento] do not produce enough to pay the salary of a corregidor." The execution of the new law would soon make this fact patent, when his Majesty's revenues would diminish and the country would be abandoned, a process which had already begun.

In the treatment of the natives the conscience of his Majesty is well acquitted, and that of your Highness may rest easy, because everything is being done [for them]. It is not allowed to collect excessive tribute from them, or to treat them ill, or to use them as carriers against their will; and so much attention is being given to the matter that no Spaniard now dares to harm an Indian. On the contrary, the natives are so favored that they dare to mistreat the Spaniards, not giving them anything to eat except for money and at high prices, and only when they wish and not when the Spaniards request and need it. There are alguaciles among them who dare to arrest a Spaniard and tie him up and bring him before this Audiencia. . . . They know how to file complaints about anything at all, and, when they see that they are given more credence than the Spaniards, at times wrongly, and when they learn that for any small matter of mistreating an Indian they can destroy the one who does it, things are no longer what they

used to be, but everything is in such good order that it could not be more so. For this reason the natives are masters of their estates and many of them are rich, and all of them have what their forefathers never had, so much so that all the money in the country belongs to them, because they own all the provisions and sell them at such high prices that no one can live in this country. A hundredweight (*fanega*) of wheat sells for a peso, and it cannot be had; maize for half a peso. . . . They raise, sell, and traffic in cattle and silk, in such quantities that there is a town in the Mixteca where the natives produce [yearly] for themselves 2,000 pounds of silk, and they pay in tributes only 900 pesos in gold dust.

The replies of the Franciscan friars of Mexico City, of Francisco Terrazas, a prominent encomendero, and of Presbyter Gómez Maraver of New Galicia all repeated substantially the same arguments against the abolition of the encomienda and need not be summarized.

Once Tello de Sandoval had consented to a temporary suspension of the New Laws affecting the encomiendas, a delegation was immediately chosen by the encomenderos to plead their case before the Council of the Indies. The delegates were Jerónimo López and Alonso de Villanueva. The three religious orders were represented by Francisco de Soto, for the Franciscans; Domingo de la Cruz, for the Dominicans; Juan de San Román, for the Augustinians. They left for Spain on June 17, 1544.

A year later the delegates of the encomenderos presented a lengthy and wellreasoned petition, the arguments of which repeated the testimony given in reply to Tello de Sandoval's interrogatory. They urged two measures: (1) the immediate suspension of the New Laws; (2) the perpetual encomienda. They rang again the familiar changes of the argument for the encomienda, but their conclusion had weight. The encomenderos, they said, were the ones who, in the expectation of perpetuity and succession, had thus far supported the country, but now that they saw the New Laws driving them from their homes, they were saving what they could in order to return to Spain, preferring to return poor to waiting until they and their wives should be killed, because if they should abandon the land the Indians would seize it.

The Council of the Indies faced the undeniable fact that the New Laws would have to be amended if serious trouble in the colonies was to be avoided. One member handed down an opinion generally supporting the defenders of the encomienda. In short, he approved of the encomienda, but he suggested that its evils might be mitigated by a more careful selection of the men to whom it was granted and by certain additional restrictions: (1) The tribute should be fixed at a moderate sum and adjusted from time to time. (2) No personal services should be required of the Indians, save moderate work on farms at a small wage. (3) In assessing the tribute a small amount, say one-twentieth, should be set aside for the King. (4) The oidores should visit the encomiendas, with or without complaints from the Indians. If the encomenderos should be found to be mistreating them their encomiendas should be incorporated in the Crown.

Two strong voices were raised in favor of retaining the New Laws unchanged, Sebastián Ramírez de Fuenleal and, of course, Bartolomé de las Casas. The rest of the Council of the Indies may have encouraged the delegates from New Spain to go directly to the Emperor at Malines in Belgium, where they persuaded him to repeal Article 35, which abolished the encomienda upon the death of its present holder. It was, however, only a qualified victory for the encomenderos. The law restricting the succession of the encomienda to one heir remained in force, although it was never rigidly applied; the encomenderos were deprived of the privileges of using the labor of the Indians (i.e., of considering the personal services of the Indians as tributes), of taking slaves, and of using the Indians as carriers. These measures were, to be sure, modified from time to time as necessity dictated, but it was evident from this point on that the encomenderos enjoyed their privileges only on a permissive basis. As the second generation grew old, the question of the succession of the encomienda and its escheating to the Crown came up again, and eventually led to the unlucky conspiracy of the Avila brothers in 1566.

Meanwhile, Mendoza had his hands full trying to enforce the New Laws affecting personal service and Indian slavery. Petitioners against the abolition of slavery argued that it was unjust to penalize the men who had acquired their slaves by purchase, and that mining could not be carried on without them. One petition was read to the Council of the Indies by Bernal Díaz del Castillo, who was acting as a delegate of the encomenderos of Guatemala. The enslavement of rebellious Indians was left to the discretion of the Audiencia by a cédula of 1549. It seems likely that the Council of the Indies was persuaded to keep slaving as a punitive measure by the dangerous rebellion of the Maya in Yucatan, in 1546–1547. At the same time, the encomenderos were forbidden to use their Indians in the mines, and the Audiencia was directed to prevent the commutation of tributes into services in the mines. The New Law concerning Indian carriers was soon modified to permit their use where there was a shortage of pack animals, but their loads were to be moderate and their journeys short. The Council also decided that the present wage of carriers amounted to their working for nothing, for they received 8½ maravedís (equivalent to ¼ real, or 1⁄32 peso) a day. It reminded the Audiencia that it was the ultimate purpose of the Crown to abolish personal services entirely.

The viceroy analyzed the carrier and personal service question with his usual realism. He suspected, he wrote the Council of the Indies, that the law forbidding the use of carriers had been adopted on the advice of people who did not know the facts. The stories of the abuse of carriers had been exaggerated. Carriers were needed to take supplies to the new mines of

Zacatecas, for there were not enough pack animals by one-twentieth to handle the traffic. In fact, there was no way to travel in New Spain without carriers for one's personal effects. The missionaries were to use them, and even Tello de Sandoval had been forced to transgress the law in this respect. Indian merchants were allowed to use carriers without restriction, and thus they were gaining an unfair advantage over their Spanish competitors. Military expeditions were impossible without carriers, and if government officials were obliged to rent pack animals every time they went from one place to another their entire salaries would not suffice to cover the cost of a single trip. After all, a fifty-pound load was no heavier for an Indian than it was for a Spaniard. Now, wherever a Spaniard went he was held up by some corregidor, scale in hand, to discover whether his Indians were carrying two or three pounds above the prescribed load. Indian merchants had to suffer no such annoyance.

Mendoza thought that the laws against the use of carriers and against personal services might work some benefit in New Spain if he were allowed to use his discretion in their application. The Spaniards, he reminded the Council, had not invented personal services, which had been customary among the Indians since time immemorial. Their whole system of government depended upon personal services, and even the Spanish system could not dispense with them. It was absurd to make services voluntary, even for wages, because the Indians would not work for the Spaniards unless forced to do so. And now that the slaves had been freed, the mines could not be worked because Negro slaves were too expensive. Also, the new industries, which were manned by natives, would all be ruined if made dependent upon voluntary labor.

Now that the first enthusiasm for reform had cooled off a bit, the Council of the Indies, impressed by the reasoning of Mendoza and the rest, adopted a less magisterial attitude. Mendoza was undoubtedly in the right, for the government of New Spain could not function without forced services of one kind or another. The Council decreed that carriers might be used, but they were to be hired in the presence of royal officers, who were to fix the weight to be carried, the wages, the length of journeys, and to issue licenses. No mestizo who was not the legitimate son of a Spaniard might use carriers. It also decided that, although government officials had been forbidden to use carriers, the government itself could not be so restricted. The new cathedral of Michoacán was to be completed by subscription: the Crown would bear a third of the cost (out of the tributes of the Indians), the encomenderos a third (*idem*), and the Indians a third.

There was considerable literary activity in the Council of the Indies during the closing years of Mendoza's reign. One long cédula reviewed the whole question of the encomienda and forced services and showed the Council to be still impaled upon its ancient dilemma. It seems that certain encomenderos had objected to having religious in their encomiendas, so the Audiencia was directed to see that the religious were free to go where they pleased and erect monasteries. Carriers might be relieved by the building of roads and bridges. Indians held at the mines against their will were to be released, but the Audiencia might not allow them to remain idle. Cattle were to be kept away from the Indians' *milpas*. Sites were to be chosen for Spanish towns where no harm would come to the Indians from them. The New Laws, except those which had been repealed, were to be enforced. The Audiencia might mitigate the vagabond nuisance by putting the offenders to work or by exiling a few of them by way of example. Crown officers were again reminded that they were forbidden to use Indians in personal service.

Bishop Zárate's complaint about the corregidores, or others like it, brought a cédula forbidding these officials to collect the tribute, which thereafter was to be handled by an officer appointed for the purpose — another dead letter. Native overseers (calpisques) hired by encomenderos and corregidores were to be examined in the future for good character before being licensed.

The illicit traffic in Indian slaves proved difficult to control because of the shortage of labor in the mines and the high prices commanded by the slaves (up to forty pesos). A typical remedy suggested by the Council of the Indies was that the Audiencia should appoint the Franciscans as the special guardians of Indian slaves. The Audiencia would then appoint a prosecutor to handle the cases of abuse reported by the guardians.

That Mendoza no longer considered the encomienda to be a problem may be gathered from his failure to mention it in his instructions to his successor, Luis de Velasco. The New Laws had, indeed, purged it of its most notorious fault, the power to coerce labor, and had taken from the encomendero his quasi-feudal independence, reducing him to the status of a pensioner of the Crown. He received the tributes of the Indians entrusted to him, he looked (presumably) after their welfare, and in return for his privileges he acted as militiaman when necessary. In reality the Crown was now the only encomendero in the old sense, because it alone had the power to assess tributes and to coerce labor "for the good of the state."

THE NEW LAWS—ANOTHER ANALYSIS

LEWIS HANKE

Lewis Hanke (1905–   ) has devoted much of his very productive scholarly life to the investigation and interpretation of the official efforts of the Spaniards to regulate and humanize relationships between their sons overseas and the American peoples whom their sons conquered. His work has led him to study the majestic figure of Bartolomé de Las Casas and to bring this famous Dominican to the full notice of American readers. Hanke's undergraduate and early graduate studies were done at Northwestern; his doctorate was granted by Harvard, in 1936. From 1939 to 1951 he was the Director of the Hispanic Foundation of the Library of Congress; the next ten years he spent at the University of Texas; in 1961 he was called to fill the chair of Latin American History at Columbia University. The selection here is from his work which was awarded the Beveridge Prize of the American Historical Association in 1947.

THE fourth and last great experiment undertaken by Spaniards in the first half-century of their conquest was the most daring of all, and the one least likely to succeed. The colonization attempt of Las Casas had failed, the experiments to test the capacity of the Indians had not discovered any natives able to live alone as free subjects of the King, but the preaching of the faith by peaceful means alone was pro-

From Lewis Hanke, *The Spanish Struggle for Justice in the Conquest of America* (Philadelphia: University of Pennsylvania Press, for the American Historical Association, 1949), pp. 83–105. Reprinted by permission of the University of Pennsylvania Press.

ceeding well — at least in 1542. On November 20 of that year, Emperor Charles V cast aside the advice of some of his oldest and most important advisers and, following the recommendations of Las Casas and other Dominicans that the encomienda system be abolished, promulgated the famous New Laws. These New Laws revoked or limited the right of Spaniards to service and tribute from Indians, who would ultimately be put under the crown and administered by paid royal officials along with the other natives known as "crown Indians." This radical step led to a near revolt in Mexico, a serious rebellion in Peru in which the Viceroy was killed, and provoked grave unrest throughout the empire. Why did the Emperor approve these New Laws?

To Bartolomé de Las Casas, whose constant and vociferous efforts on behalf of the Indians were largely responsible for the passage of these laws, the answer was simple and clear. The existence of the encomienda made invalid the just title of the king of Spain to the Indies, and stigmatized him as a tyrant instead of a true lord, for true lordship required either that the people of the land spontaneously subject themselves to the rule of Spain or that the King, given jurisdiction over them at the behest of the Pope, use it for the sole purpose of benefiting those people. The encomienda system, which virtually enslaved the Indians according to Las Casas, was from no point of view beneficial to them. Therefore, since it negated the king's just title, it must be wiped out. . . .

THE DEVELOPMENT OF THE ENCOMIENDA
SYSTEM TO 1542

The early regulations drawn up for the encomienda and its official sanction in 1512 under the Laws of Burgos have been already described as specific results of the first cry for justice in America by Friar Antonio de Montesinos. The Burgos regulations were extremely precise and humane, but they proved unenforceable. The fruitless Jeronymite rule of 1518 followed, succeeded in turn by more disputes, more

meetings in Spain. By now Las Casas had entered the battle and had impressed upon the King's preachers the miserable condition of the Indians, and the injustice and evil effects of the encomienda system. Miguel de Salamanca, the oldest and most authoritative of the preachers, presented a memorial which has been preserved in the *History of the Indies* of Las Casas. This statement contains the substance of all the subsequent attacks against the encomienda.

The greatest evil which has caused the total destruction of those lands and which will continue, unless a remedy be found, and which is neither just nor can it or ought it be allowed in reason, is the encomienda of the Indians as it now exists, that is to say, being allotted for life in order that, working as they are worked, all the profit deriving from their work goes to those who hold them in encomienda; wherefore this form of encomienda and the manner in which it is executed is contrary to the well-being of the Indian Republic; also it is against all reason and human prudence; also it is against the welfare and service of our Lord the King and contrary to all civil and canon law; also it is against all rules of moral philosophy and theology; also it is against God and his will and his Church.

Although the Council received this memorial civilly, and the King, on May 20, 1520, decreed that the Indians ought to be free and be treated as freemen, the memorial does not appear to have had any direct effect. It is true that in 1523, the King ordered Cortés not to commend Indians "because God created the Indians free and not subject," but this law was not obeyed and, after many discussions, the encomienda was legalized in 1526 for New Spain, with the proviso that no encomendero was to receive more than three hundred Indians.

When the first audiencia was sent to Mexico in 1528, the crown offered to make encomiendas permanent and to give the Spanish holders lordship and jurisdiction over the Indians in a certain form that was to be stated at the time of making the grants. The crown veered around sharply during the next two years, and in 1530 gave the second audiencia strict instructions to establish the office of corregidor, a royal official who was to administer Indians placed under the crown. The crown's promise of 1528 was not redeemed, although petitions by conquistadores for formal grants of Indian fiefs poured into the court continuously.

The disputes continued, although Las Casas during these years was living quietly in a convent in Hispaniola and the battle was carried on by other Indian defenders.

The stoutest opponent of the encomienda system at the time was the Bishop of Santo Domingo, Sebastián Ramírez de Fuenleal, who was later to take part in the great battle of the New Laws in 1542. Now as president of the Audiencia of New Spain he recommended that royal officials be put in charge of the Indians and that conquistadores be given a regular pension. If the encomenderos complained that the land would therefore be depopulated and lost to the crown, Bishop Ramírez advised the Empress on February 2, 1533, she could safely disregard such predictions, for Spaniards desirous of encomiendas had been making them since the conquest began.

The advice of this principal royal official in New Spain was not followed. Shortly after the conclusion of the last experiencia in Cuba, in 1536, the famous Law of Inheritance for Two Generations was passed, which permitted encomenderos to pass on their encomiendas as inheritance to their legitimate descendants or to their widows for one life. The law thus encouraged the hope that a permanent inheritance for the conquistadores and their families might soon be secured. Now voices were raised for grants in perpetuity, and even for a law which would hand over to the Spaniards, forever, civil and criminal jurisdiction over the Indians. Just at this juncture Las Casas arrived in Spain, fresh from the triumphs of peaceful preaching in the Land of True Peace in Guatemala, and determined that an even greater triumph must be achieved:

the encomienda system itself must be destroyed.

THE "EIGHTH REMEDY" OF LAS CASAS AND HIS "VERY BRIEF ACCOUNT OF THE DESTRUCTION OF THE INDIES"

These were years of great ferment in Spain on Indian affairs. The bull of Pope Paul III, declaring the Indians free and capable of receiving the faith, had just been issued. The problem of the basis for the just title of the king of Spain to the Indies was being aired throughout the land, and so many memorials and treatises were written on the subject that the King "was discomfited thereby."

Las Casas reached Spain in 1539 determined, according to one author, either to win real assistance for the Indians or to abandon his work for them to labor in other mission fields. It was at this time that his denunciation of the slapdash methods used by some ecclesiastics to baptize thousands of Indians without proper religious instruction so disturbed the court that the noted Friar Francisco de Vitoria and some of the other foremost theologians of Salamanca were called upon to render an opinion on the matter.

Las Casas was more concerned, however, to make sure that there would be Indians left to baptize. For two years he haunted the court and Council of the Indies, advocating the abolition of the encomienda system, which he believed to be the principal enemy of the Indians. The President of the Council, Cardinal Loaysa, remained unmoved by the charges and denunciations of Las Casas. Emperor Charles V was absent from Spain during this period, but returned in 1542, and almost immediately ordered that special meetings be held to consider Indian matters, an action which some believed was caused by Las Casas' influence with the Emperor's Flemish advisers. During the years 1542 and 1543 Las Casas was much at court, seems to have had a hand in all decisions of the Council of the Indies, and as usual composed two special treatises to forward his cause.

The first treatise was entitled *Remedies for the Existing Evils, with Twenty Reasons Therefor,* a stern condemnation of the whole encomienda system.

In this juridical treatise, the following propositions were the most significant ones:

The pope intended to do the Indians a favor, not harm, by his donation to the king of Spain. The Indians are free, and do not lose this liberty by becoming vassals to the king of Spain. Inasmuch as the Indies are far away, no partial prohibition of encomiendas or attempts to regulate them by law will succeed. A general order must be issued, in such wise that it cannot be contravened.

The other treatise written by Las Casas during these years was the famous — or infamous — *Very Brief Account of the Destruction of the Indies.* This denunciation of Spanish treatment of the Indians caused oceans of words to flow in the sixteenth and succeeding centuries, including our own. This bloody description of the Spanish conquest, translated into all the principal European languages and illustrated with gruesome pictures, served as the choicest weapon of anti-Spanish propagandists everywhere. Even today it seems to have a Lorelei-like attraction for Hispanophiles who wish to combat the black legend of Spanish cruelty in America, and the revisionists quote Las Casas so frequently in their attacks on his writings that they help to spread ever more widely his accusations.

At once there sprang up persons to challenge Las Casas' statistics — for he claimed some fifteen or twenty millions of Indians had perished — and to complain that he gave a most unbalanced picture of Spanish deeds in the New World in the first half-century after Columbus. His vehemence in 1542 has been matched by the vehemence of other Spaniards who have been denouncing him these four hundred years.

It is not possible to present here an essay on the comparative cruelty of Europeans in America which would do justice to this large theme. No one today would defend the statistics Las Casas gave, but few would deny that there was considerable truth in his main charges. One Mexican writer, who has devoted himself to analyzing the *Very Brief Account,* concludes that the detractors of Las Casas have shrewdly exploited his numerical errors without ever disproving his essential truths.

Other Spaniards than Las Casas charged their countrymen with cruelty. The secret investigation against Viceroy Antonio de Mendoza contained this accusation:

After the capture of the hill of Mixtón, many of the Indians taken in the conquest of the said hill were put to death in his presence and by his orders. Some were placed in line and blown into bits by cannon fire; others were torn to pieces by dogs; and others were given to Negroes to be put to death, and these killed them with knife thrusts, while others were hung. Again, at other places, Indians were thrown to the dogs in his presence.

Friar Motolinía, certainly no friend of Las Casas and author of one of the bitterest and most sarcastic letters ever written against him, stated in the *History of the Indians of New Spain* that "countless" natives were destroyed in labor at the mines, that service in the mines of Oaxyecac was so destructive that for half a league around it the Spaniards could not walk except on dead men or bones, and that so many birds came to scavenge that they darkened the sky. The royal official Alonso de Zurita stated that he had heard many Spaniards say that in Popayán province the bones of dead Indians were so thick along the roads that one could never lose the way. Governor Francisco de Castañeda in Nicaragua reported that Spaniards on horseback hunted down Indians and lanced them, including women and children, at the slightest provocation or with no provocation whatsoever.

The historian Pedro Cieza de León, who participated in the Peruvian campaigns, wrote:

I know from my experience gathered during a long residence in the Indies that there were great cruelties and much injury done to the natives, such as cannot be lightly stated. All know how populous the island of Hispaniola was, and that if the Christians had treated the natives decently and as friends there would certainly be many there now. Yet there remains no other testimony of the country having once been peopled than the great cemeteries of the dead, and the ruins of the places where they lived. In Tierra Firme and Nicaragua also not an Indian is left. They asked Belalcázar how many he found between Quito and Cartago, and they desired to know from me how many now remain. Well, there are none. In a town which had a population of ten thousand Indians there was not one. When we came from Cartagena with Vadillo I saw a Portuguese, named Roque Martín, who had quarters of Indians hanging on a perch to feed his dogs with, as if they were those of wild beasts. In the Realm of New Granada and in Popayán they did things so ruthless that I would rather not mention them.

Some of the most telling descriptions of Spanish cruelty were embedded in royal orders, so much so that the seventeenth-century jurist Solórzano was ordered to remove from the manuscript of his *Política Indiana* some of the royal orders on mistreatment of Indians to prevent notice of these things reaching foreigners. Anyone who reads widely in the chronicles and reports left by Spaniards will find information supporting and supplementing many of the accusations made by Las Casas in 1542.

The diseases brought by Spaniards took heavy toll of the Indians, the dislocation of Indian life and customs caused grave difficulties, as any anthropologist today would expect and as Las Casas realized in the sixteenth century, and the filthy habits of the Spaniards may have also helped to destroy the bath-taking natives of the New World.

There appears to have existed in Europe, long before Las Casas wrote, a disposition to believe in the cruelty of Spaniards in their conquests. About 1522, for example, a short anonymous account of Yucatán appeared in German with a woodcut which shows three evil-looking men dressed like Europeans engaged in chopping up babies. And the cosmography of Sebastian Münster has an American scene depicting a man and woman dismembering a human being on a table, while another cut shows the man sitting comfortably on a stool beside a slow fire, over which he turns a spit thrust through a headless body. The famous De Bry illustrations, which spread far and wide the denunciations of Las Casas even to those who could not read, therefore had predecessors which tended to paint the same dark picture of Spanish action in the New World.

The above recital of gruesome details is not made to blacken the history of Spain in America or to add soot to the black legend, but rather to provide necessary background for a consideration of the New Laws, the ordinances by which Charles V tried to abolish the encomienda system. Certainly one of the documents which helped to produce an atmosphere in which it was possible to secure royal approval for such a radical innovation was the *Very Brief Account of the Destruction of the Indies*. As Antonio de León Pinelo emphasized in his *Tratado de confirmaciones reales*, an impressive seventeenth-century treatise dedicated to the task of proving the justice of the encomienda system, the bad treatment of the Indians by the Spaniards was the cause of the whole dispute. And to those who denounce Las Casas as an "insensate fanatic," who singlehanded destroyed Spain's reputation, the conclusion of the late Pelham Box still is a valid answer:

The implication that but for the Apostle of the Indians Spain would have escaped the hostility of jealous neighbors is too naïve to be discussed. No power possessing a rich empire can hope to escape envy. . . . If he [Las Casas] exaggerated on details he was right in fundamentals and his truth is not affected by the use hypocritical foreigners made of his works. . . . It is not the least of Spain's glories that she produced Bartolomé de Las Casas and actually listened to him, however ineffectively.

THE NEW LAWS

The "Laws and ordinances newly made by His Majesty for the government of the Indies and good treatment and preservation of the Indians," formally approved by Charles V at Barcelona on November 20, 1542, have been, as Henry Stevens declared, "at once the pride and humiliation of Spain," and merit detailed description. They include the first regulations to establish procedures for the Council of the Indies, as well as ordinances on the Indians.

The individual laws provided for such matters as that the Council of the Indies should meet every day, that the servants of the President or Council members should not be attorneys or officials before the court, that those officers should not accept bribes or engage in private business, that they should take especial care for the preservation and increase of the Indians, and also laid down a number of specific rules on the conduct of business that came before the Council.

Then follow detailed regulations so sweeping and so strongly in favor of the Indians that Las Casas himself might well have drafted them. The audiencias were commanded "to enquire continually into the excesses and ill treatment which are or shall be done to them by governors or private persons, and how the ordinances and instructions which have been given to them and are made for the good treatment of the said Indians have been observed." It was further commanded "that henceforward, for no cause of war nor any other cause whatsoever, though it be under title of rebellion, nor by ransom nor in any other manner can an Indian be made a slave, and we desire that they be treated as of the Crown of Castile, since such they are." Indians "who until now have been enslaved against all reason and right" were to be put at liberty. Indians were not to carry loads unless absolutely necessary and then only "in such a manner that no risk of life or health of the said Indians may ensue." No free Indian was to be taken to the pearl fisheries against his will, "for since these fisheries have not been conducted in a proper manner, deaths of many Indians and Negroes have ensued."

Most grievous of all, in the estimation of the conquistadores, were the provisions regarding encomiendas. Those who held Indians without proper title were to lose them; those who held unreasonable numbers of Indians in Mexico — and these persons were listed by name — were to have some taken away, and those who had ill-treated their Indians were to be deprived of them, especially "those principal persons" involved in the disturbances of Pizarro and Almagro in Peru. The climax was reached, for the encomenderos, by the laws taking Indians away from all royal officials and prelates, and prohibiting all future grants of Indians. As it was stipulated in Law No. 35, "Henceforth no encomienda is to be granted to anyone, and when the present holders of encomiendas die, their Indians will revert to the crown."

Indians thus taken away and put under the crown were to be well treated and instructed, and the first conquistadores and married settlers were to be preferred in appointments to royal offices in the Indies. New discoveries were to be made according to certain rigid rules, no Indians were to be brought back as loot, and the tribute to be assessed on newly discovered natives would be fixed by the Governor. Finally, Indians of the islands of San Juan, Cuba, and Hispaniola "are not to be molested with demands for tribute, or other services . . . but must be treated in the same manner as the Spaniards who reside in the said islands."

The reaction of rage and astonishment among the conquistadores was instantaneous and inevitable, for by these laws the property of every encomendero was diminished and the future of his family made insecure. All the most powerful officials, royal and ecclesiastical alike, were similarly disadvantaged. It was particularly galling to the colonial Spaniards who, as encomenderos, had developed secure and honored positions in the New World, that the Spaniards at home should have contrived these laws which, if enforced, would reduce the position and security of the very men who, in their own opinion, had contributed most to Spain's glory in the New World.

WHY WERE THE NEW LAWS DECREED?

No ordinance Spain passed for the government of the Indians was more important than the New Laws, yet we do not know the full story of their enactment and their revision. Certain manuscript records have recently been found, however, which throw some light on these significant events in the history of America. These manuscripts contain the opinions of nearly all the members of the junta before the New Laws were passed, and also given by the same advisers before they were revoked. They embody, therefore, the attitudes of the Emperor's principal advisers before and after the event.

An analysis of these opinions shows the majority of junta members definitely opposed to the encomienda system as then functioning, although a minority made various counterproposals and the experienced President of the Council of the Indies voted against the hasty abolition of the system.

It must be emphasized that Las Casas was not the only friar agitating at this time for reform in the Indies. The Franciscan Jacobo de Testera had arrived for this same purpose in 1540 with a warm letter from Archbishop Zumárraga recommending him and Las Casas for their zeal and devotion to the protection of the Indians. The Dominicans Juan de Torres and Pedro de Angulo were also present at court working for the Indians.

The court likewise had other information on cruelty to Indians than that furnished by Las Casas in his *Very Brief Account of the Destruction of the Indies*. It appears from manuscripts in the Archivo General de Indias that one of the most respected members of the Council, Gregorio López, was sent early in 1543 to Seville to inspect the India House and make a special investigation there on the "liberty of the Indians." This document sheds little light on their liberty, but it does show that many persons were ready to depose what they knew concerning the ill-treatment being meted out all over the Indies. Here may be found the statements dated June 23, 1543, of Luis de Morales, who had earlier submitted an extensive individual report, Rodrigo Calderón, Licenciado Loaysa of the Mexican Audiencia, the Bishop of Tierra Firme, Diego Alemán, Pedro de Aguilar, and others. Spain must have rocked with complaints on cruelty to Indians, for the Spanish Cortes of 1542 in Valladolid petitioned the King to "remedy the cruelties which are committed in the Indies against the Indians to the end that God be served and the Indies preserved and not depopulated as is now the case." The royal reply was noncommittal: "We shall provide as it may be convenient," but this petition shows that some defender of the Indians must have been circulating among the representatives at the Valladolid Cortes, in that fateful year of 1542, and had left no stone unturned.

While the parliament was going on record against cruelty to Indians, and the special junta was deliberating on the abolition of the encomienda system, Charles V ordered an inspection (*visita*) of the Council of the Indies itself, which indicated that something was felt to be wrong there. Professor Ernest Schaefer, author of the standard monograph on the Council, is not certain why the visita was held, and his most diligent search has not turned up the records of this inspection. One contemporary writer asserted that Las Casas was responsible for having the visita made, but the few records existing in the archives are silent on this point. Apparently the Council was suspended from June 1542 until February 1543. During the course of the visita it was discovered that Dr. Beltrán, the oldest member, had accepted gifts of money from Cortés, Hernando Pizarro, and Diego de Almagro, for which he was fined and dismissed. The Bishop of Lugo, who opposed the abolition of the encomienda, was likewise fined, dismissed, and exiled to his bishopric. The Emperor also lost confidence in Cardinal Loaysa, President of the Council, on account of various complaints which were not made public because of his exalted position. Charles V called in the Bishop of Cuenca, Sebastián Ramírez, who was stoutly opposed to encomiendas, to assist the Cardinal in Indian affairs. The Emperor probably had been suspicious of the Council for some time, since he had received a secret report in 1541 charging that Pizarro had sent bribes to several members to win them to his side in pending disputes.

Charles V called on Las Casas and his faithful friend Friar Rodrigo de Andrada to appear before the Council, which was instructed to hear them because of their great experience and knowledge. Throughout the tense period when the New Laws were being considered, Las Casas appears to have been active and influential. The Emperor conferred another distinction on him by nominating Las Casas as bishop of Chiapa. A few months later the additions to the New Laws were made, and the complete text was printed on July 8, 1543. Las Casas' authority was now so great that, according to one account, he was responsible for the visita, and "nothing was determined in the Council except by his direction, for the Emperor had ordered that he enter the Council." His influence was such, asserted this same author, that the Emperor accepted everything that Las Casas said and was prepared to leave Peru to the Incas, until Friar Francisco de Vitoria counseled him not to do so, lest Christianity perish there.

Contemporaries saw the hand of Las Casas guiding Charles V and even winding this experienced ruler around his little finger. That the tough-minded Charles was frightened or hurried into precipitate action merely by Las Casas seems unlikely for, as the historian Ranke said, "there never was an instance of his having been forced into anything by violence or danger." The vigorous representations of Las Casas against the injustices he saw in the encomienda must have had great weight, however, with a monarch who already distrusted the Council of the Indies, whose members were accused of having accepted bribes from the lords of the Indies, these very men who stood to gain from encomiendas and were loudly clamoring for them.

Las Casas continued to press for more protection for the Indians throughout the remainder of 1543 and the early months of 1544. By spring he came to believe that their legal rights were so firmly established in Spain that his presence was no longer necessary in court. He must have known that representatives of conquistadores in Spain had hastily sent copies of the laws they hated to the New World and were grimly biding their time while waiting for the explosion they knew would come. Perhaps Las Casas expected this too and wished to be in the thick of the fight in America.

At any rate Las Casas finally decided to accept the bishopric of Chiapa, in which lay the Land of True Peace. On Passion Sunday of 1544, this veteran of the Indies was consecrated bishop in the Church of St. Paul, in the "Very Noble and Very Loyal City" of Seville. Las Casas had been born here, and now it was from this same city that he set forth at seventy years of age to continue his labor for the Indians of Chiapa. He would be among friends, for in this bishopric his Dominican brothers were successfully putting into effect one of his great dreams, preaching the faith to Indians by peaceful means alone. Behind him lay, as he thought, his most spectacular victory over the forces of selfishness and ungodliness. The New Laws had been decreed, despite all the influence the conquistadores and their friends could muster against them, and these laws foreshadowed the eventual death of the encomienda system. The Dominican friar Bartolomé de Las Casas had set in motion as revolutionary a change in American society and in the administration of Spain's great empire overseas as his contemporary Nicolaus Copernicus had achieved in astronomical circles with his *De revolutionibus orbium coelestium,* printed in the same year as the New Laws.

THE ENCOMIENDA IS NOT ABOLISHED AFTER ALL

The ink was scarcely dry on the printed New Laws before the Franciscan Jacobo de Testera was back in Mexico informing the Indians of the great victory won by himself, Las Casas, and other champions of the Indian cause at court. The City Council discussed in solemn session on July 23, 1543, the disturbing news that

the French Franciscan Jacobo de Testera had arrived from Castile, and had permitted a great multitude of Indians to come out to receive him. These Indians bestowed gifts upon him and performed other services, erecting triumphal arches, sweeping clean the streets he was to pass and strewing upon them cyperus and roses, and bearing him upon a litter — all this because he and other Franciscans had informed the Indians that they had come to free the Indians and restore them to the state they enjoyed before they were placed under the rule of the King of Spain. These statements had excited the Indians and they went forth to receive Friar Testera as though he were a viceroy.

The hopes of the Indians must have faded almost as quickly as the roses with which they welcomed Testera bearing his glad tidings. The Visitador Tello de Sandoval, sent to Mexico to enforce the New Laws, suspended the more rigorous ones as soon as he arrived in Mexico City, on account of the tremendous protests that reached his ears. In Peru the situation was even more dangerous, since the Viceroy Blasco Núñez Vela had arrived in Lima with the New Laws just as the revolt of Gonzalo Pizarro was well under way. Benito Juárez de Carvajal captured the Viceroy himself in the battle of Anaquito, decapitated him, and carried his head by the hair until this became inconvenient, when he put a string through the lips and

thus bore it along happily, "calling it to the attention of everyone he passed."

With the Viceroy's head on a string, there was no possibility of enforcing even the current laws, much less the New Laws. Indeed, Pizarro's advisers urged him to assume the kingship of Peru, marry an Inca princess, grant encomiendas in perpetuity, and enact judicious laws for the effectual protection of the Indians. The history of this revolt is well known, and need not be repeated here.

Equally well known is the campaign waged by the Spaniards in Mexico against the New Laws. Tello de Sandoval, sent to enforce them, took down a quantity of information from royal officials, colonists, and ecclesiastics which showed that opinion was overwhelmingly against them. Perhaps most important of all, many unfavorable opinions and depositions on the matter were sent by friars of all the orders to the King and Council of the Indies. Indeed, the provincials of the Augustinians, Dominicans, and Franciscans made the long journey from Mexico to Spain to inform the King on "necessary remedies," and to demonstrate that the highest dignitaries of the missionary orders in closest contact with the Indians were solidly behind the conquistadores. The City Council of Mexico City despatched two special representatives, Alonso de Villanueva and Gonzalo López, who presented in June 1545 a long memorial advocating suspension of the New Laws and perpetuity of encomiendas. Many of these petitions, letters, and memorials have been printed and are familiar to students of this subject.

The separate opinion of the special groups convoked by the Emperor to reconsider the New Laws have not been published, however, with one exception, but are preserved in the Archives of the Indies through the diligence of some clerk who made copies of them, probably for the use of Charles V. Evidence presented directly to this group has also been preserved. A number of Spaniards fresh from Mexico gave their first-hand account of the parlous state of affairs there; one witness, Juan Díaz de Gibraleón, a merchant who had lived eight years in Mexico with his wife, had returned to Castile because of the New Laws and did not intend to risk his business further in the New World. He had himself seen more than one hundred married Spaniards likewise bring back their wives and property to Spain because, under the New Laws, conquistadores and others were not able to buy goods and business was at a standstill. Many other witnesses deposed that they had returned or would return unless the situation were remedied. One even stated that seven or eight hundred discontented persons had returned to Spain on the same ship as himself. . . .

The special representatives, Villanueva and López, also made a summary statement on June 9, reminding the King that the opinions, petitions, letters, and other statements all clearly indicated that it would be to the manifest advantage of the Indians, the King, and God that Indians be given in perpetuity to Spaniards. The various religious orders having already presented their formal opinions, these representatives felt that it was not right that individual ecclesiastics be allowed to present their views. . . .

A large body of material which the Visitor Sandoval collected from the ecclesiastics in Mexico was also abstracted and summarized for the King and Council of the Indies. . . .

The royal advisers, therefore, had a quantity of reports and information as they sat down to consider the revocation, and practically all of it was against the New Laws. . . .

All the opinions and deliberations of the royal advisers were faithfully reported by Prince Philip to Emperor Charles V, who was absent in Germany on imperial affairs. The representatives from Mexico went there, too, to press their case in person. Likewise an Augustinian friar, possibly the Provincial from Mexico, Juan de San Román, paid a personal visit to Charles which is supposed to have been instrumen-

tal in turning the tide. According to another interpretation, Charles V was offered twenty-one million *pesos de oro* for the revocation of one of the New Laws, and similar amounts for others, presumably by the representatives from Mexico. At any rate, on October 20, 1545, at Malines, Charles did revoke Law No. 35, which was the heart of the matter: it prohibited the granting of encomiendas and required all encomiendas to revert to the crown at the death of the encomendero. By this single stroke, Charles V reversed the policy he had so strongly approved less than three years before. The encomenderos won a complete victory on this vital issue, and a royal decree was also promulgated specifically reëstablishing the right of succession of their wives and children. The law requiring all suits concerning Indians to be heard by the King in person was likewise revoked, although this revocation was itself soon revised to provide that encomienda cases should go to Spain for adjudication, with the audiencias merely transmitting testimony.

But this was not all. The provincials of the three orders and one of the representatives from Mexico kept after Charles, and succeeded in persuading him to revoke, in February 1546, the law which removed Indians from encomenderos who had treated their charges badly and from persons involved in the Pizarro-Almagro fight in Peru. The New Laws relating to the encomiendas were crumbling fast, although certain provisions, such as the removal of encomiendas held by prelates, governors, and other royal officials, were carried out and the laws relating to them never repealed. The decision of the crown to continue the encomienda, however, meant that the reform group had been beaten on their most important proposal.

The aggressive delegation from Mexico was not satisfied even with this, for they desired above all to secure perpetuity for encomiendas, and continued to bombard Charles with "reasons which were just." He was now moved to act. In a most equivocal royal order of April 1546, at Ratisbon, Viceroy Antonio de Mendoza of Mexico was informed of the pressure being exerted on behalf of the encomenderos, instructed to make a careful census of the needs and merits of all conquistadores, and empowered to grant Indians, without civil or criminal jurisdiction over them, as he "saw convenient, neither more nor less than I would do if I were there, giving to every person what is proper so that all are remunerated, contented, and satisfied." Any viceroy who could have accomplished this feat in a land seething with as much discontent as Mexico would indeed have been a worthy representative of Charles V in any part of his empire! . . .

* * *

Would the New Laws have really benefited the Indians as much as Las Casas believed, if the crown had stood firm against all the pressures to change them? Would the Indians, if taken away from individual Spaniards, have been better treated under the administration of royal officials? The change would have been merely a change of masters, says Robert Levillier, the Argentine historian. Of course, no one knows the true answer to this question. We do know that the New Laws provoked the greatest battle of the century, indeed of the whole colonial period, on Indian problems, and that important ecclesiastical and lay figures felt that the enforcement of the laws would mean the ruin of the New World. It is also certain that the final decision of the crown to reverse itself and to permit the encomienda to continue not only terminated the fourth and last experiment carried on by Spaniards during the first half-century of the conquest of America — it also terminated the period of experimentation in Indian affairs. No further attempt was made to change radically the basic laws and basic institutions that had been established in these fateful fifty years. . . .

THE FRANCISCAN ATTACK ON THE REPARTIMIENTO SYSTEM (1585)

RICHARD STAFFORD POOLE

Father R. Stafford Poole, C.M. (1930–　) trained for the priesthood at the Vincentian Fathers' House of Studies, Perryville, Missouri. His graduate work was done at Saint Louis University, where he received his Ph.D. in 1961. He served for half a dozen years in the Department of History at Cardinal Glennon College, Saint Louis, and presently is on leave for another assignment. He has continued his research into this third and other provincial councils of Mexican churchmen during the colonial period; in the process he is uncovering many valuable and little-known aspects of the social and religious history of New Spain. Several short articles have been published and a major study is under preparation.

This present selection is Poole's summary and running commentary on the lengthy memorial which the Franciscans prepared for the Third Provincial Council (1585). The question of the *repartimiento*, along with many other bits of business, was on the agenda. Here is the Franciscan argument against the practice, the friars' attempt to prome it *"illicito, malo, y lleno de crueldad."*

The Franciscan Memorial

THE Franciscans, who were the leaders in the fight against the repartimientos and who were ultimately responsible for their regulation, are well represented at the Council. Indeed, the Franciscan memorial to the Council on the subject of the repartimientos is not only the longest and most detailed, but also the most theological in its approach. The Franciscans, represented here by Fray Pedro de San Sebastián, Fray Pedro Orozco, Fray Diego Vengel and Fray Juan Ramírez, did not consider the question of forced labor entirely from the point of view of the abuses involved. For them the question was entirely moral, one of justice. Consequently, their condemnation is all the more sweeping, their indictment

the more damning, and their reasoning the more profound. The repartimiento is a monstrous moral injustice which must be uprooted immediately.

The document is signed by the friars mentioned, but is undated and does not contain any of Salcedo's usual explanatory notes. It seems safe to say that it was probably presented to the Council at the same time as the others. It is preceded by a title which explains its purpose.

In the name of the Lord, and under the correction of those who know better, there follow the answers to doubts, which the Holy Synod requests of the Order of (Friars) Minor about the repartimiento of the Indians.

From Richard Stafford Poole, C.M., "The Indian Problem in the Third Provincial Council of Mexico, 1585" (an unpublished Ph.D. dissertation, Saint Louis University, 1961), pp. 187–226. Reprinted by permission of the author.

The doubts are then presented and each answered in turn.

The first is the same as that of the summary, i.e., whether the Indians can be used by clerics and ecclesiastics and other persons in works from which these employers draw personal gain, by way of business or industry. However, the doubt has that important second part, not emphasized in the original summary, but here made the burden of most of the memorial, to wit, ". . . and if all this (viz., the various abuses) should be removed, and the aforesaid repartimiento reduced to public usefulness, whether it is *per se* a good and licit moral act or not."

The answer to this last is a resounding negative, for the repartimiento is "illicito, y malo, y lleno de crueldad."

To prove this, the author of the memorial first cites the basis on which the repartimientos are usually licit. (1) The Spaniards have sunk roots in the land and become adjusted to it, both for the good of the land itself and for the conversion and Christianity of the Indians. (2) These same Spaniards must be supported, and (3) the Indians must be removed from their natural laziness, as, it is said, Montezuma himself advised Cortes.

None of these three reasons has any basis in fact. (1) The Spaniards have truly sunk roots in the new world, but only to subjugate the Indians and to take the best and most profitable lands and to live off the land in ease and plenty. (2) If the Spaniards used one half the diligence in work, that they use in forcing the Indians to work for them, the commonwealth would be far better off. Further, the Indians would then be free to cultivate their own fields of wheat and corn and the country would have a better supply of these, and they would cost less. If the Spaniards would cultivate their own lands as much as possible and leave the Indians to hire out as they can, the common good of the nation would be better achieved. In addition, there are multitudes of Vagabond Spaniards, mulattoes, mestizos, who could take their place. At the present time, they are doing nothing for the country or the common good. (3) Nor does this have any value, since the works of the repartimiento are excessive and are destroying the Indians. If they were left to cultivate their own small milpas, they would be well enough occupied.

Having disposed of the reasons brought forth to support the lawfulness of the repartimientos, the author now attempts to show that they are in themselves unlawful and immoral.

The repartimientos are iniquitous because the mulattoes, mestizos and lazy Spaniards are not forced to work, while the Indians must, merely because they are Indians (*no mas de por ser indios*). These are the same Indians who pay tribute to the King and who serve his communities, and who are also forced to leave their homes and families for work in which they often fall sick and die. This was for a people "who afflict them and treat them worse than if they were slaves." This is a "manifiesta yniquidad" and all the worse because the Indians are little better than children who are too timorous and afraid to put up resistance.

It would be good for the Spaniards to consider the natural law of "Do unto others. . ." and to reflect on how it would be if strangers occupied Spain and treated the Spaniards in a similar manner.

Another reason for the injustice of the repartimiento is the manner in which it is carried out. It is "as if men would walk out to gather herds of sheep and would go and allot and entrust them into the hands of wolves, so that these could take them to their dens." Some Spaniards treat the Indians in a Christian manner, most do not. They act as though the native workers were slaves, taken in honest warfare; they beat them on the journey and call them dogs and other worse names. When they arrive at the residences of the Spaniards, the only hospitality they receive is to have the Negroes and servants steal their food and clothes (on the pretext that thus they will not run away), and lock them in pigsties and make them work day and night, feast day or not. This is so unendurable that many Indians prefer to flee without their pay or clothes.

Of all the repartimientos, the worst is that to the mines. This must be avoided "under pain of eternal condemnation." Not even the infidels, however much they hated the Christians and tortured them, condemned them to this type of punishment. And because the Indians are delicate "to send them to the mines is nothing else than to send them to die, as experience shows" and of those who do go to the mines, "one tenth of them at least stay there dead or return [only] to die." And this while the mine operators excuse their own slaves from the worse work in order to conserve their strength. How much more ought they to do so to free men who are also the vassals of the King, who has an obligation in their regard.

For their defense, there is the *juez de repartimiento* who is charged with their protection and who is supposed to vindicate them. "We say that he is the best executioner that they have." This is simply because he receives his "certum quid" for every Indian given to service, even if they are not necessary for the various towns, and therefore he also harasses and pursues the rulers of these towns as if they were his slaves. And what of vindication of the Indian ill treated by the Spaniards? They care little, for the Spaniard "is little grieved by the work of the Indian, and he has his eye only on how he can make a profit off their sweat and service."

The fourth reason for the injustice of the repartimiento "as used at the present time" is that, instead of being necessary and useful for the Spanish nation and commonwealth, it is prejudicial and harmful. For if the Indian population is wiped out, then the Spaniards will be lost also, for they cannot subsist without the Indians. Experience has shown that when plague has depleted the Indians or kept them from work, the Spaniard has been lost. "Because they [the Spaniards] do everything by the hand

and with the help of the Indians." And again: "This is an infallible truth, that the repartimiento in the form in which it is now practiced is imperceptibly destroying the Indians, if it be not remedied."

The fifth reason is that it brings harm to the patrimony of the King of Spain and could eventually result in harm even to the royal crown. First, because the King gains much from the Indians (e.g., taxes) and secondly, without the Indians there could possibly be a revolt against the royal authority. When Indians are easily had, then men of little judgment are satisfied and while saying that there are Indians in abundance, they are ready to make common cause with Spaniards loyal to the King in order to prevent unruly spirits from making trouble. But without the Indians (who will be destroyed if the repartimiento keeps up), all the unruly elements of New Spain — Spanish, Negro, mulatto, mestizo — could cause lawlessness, riot and robbery.

The sixth reason is a most remarkable anticipation of the Black Legend and merits extensive quotation.

The sixth is that it is an obvious truth that if this repartimiento is not stopped, it will be the cause of the destruction of the Indians, of which the result will be the dishonor and perpetual infamy of our Catholic Monarchs of Spain and of the entire Spanish nation. For what greater infamy can endure for the Spanish nation during the next centuries than to say, that by its greed and cruelty, (it) destroyed and devastated a new world of innumerable and docile peoples, whom God put in their hands so that they might care for them as children, protect them and put them on the road to the salvation of their souls? And the kings and princes who consent to such a thing, what Christianity and fear of God could they have had?

The seventh reason is that the repartimiento endangers the conscience of the monarch in whose reign it takes place, for he will have to make a most strict accounting. He could incur danger to his eternal salvation, the danger most to be feared.

With the eighth, the author concludes

that the worst of all the effects of the repartimiento is that which is prejudicial to the Catholic faith, because it makes the very name Christian odious to the Indians, just as it has been to the baptized Moors of Spain.

In conclusion, he asks again if those Indians, who are intended to be used for public purposes (as in the harvests) can be used by ecclesiastics, employers or miners for particular uses.

I say that this is more illicit and more unjust, according to that maxim of the Philosopher: si id quod minus videtur in esse, inest, et quod magis videtur, inierit. If the repartimiento is for the service of the universal good and the maintenance of the commonwealth, if this we consider evil and unjust, how much worse will we hold the same repartimiento for the profit and the interests of particular persons who wish to enrich themselves with the blood and sweat of these poor natives . . .

The memorial now deals at length with all the various possible objections that could be brought against any abolition or moderation of the current system of repartimientos. It bears the title, "Answer to some objections that can be brought against this opinion." It goes on to list eight objections, some of which are repetitious, but which are a fascinating catalogue of the ways in which the sixteenth century Spaniard sought to justify his parasite-like dependence on the forced labor of the Indian. In many ways they are reminiscent of the desperate arguments advanced to justify slavery in the pre-bellum South.

FIRST OBJECTION

The first and probably the most common is an objection which, for its Social Darwinism, would have done credit to Herbert Spencer or William Graham Sumner.

As God our Lord sustains some creatures and preserves their life and being with harm to and loss of other inferior and less noble ones, according to the dictum of Aristotle, "the corruption of one thing is the generation of another," since we see that, in order that grass may grow, elements corrupt, in the same way, the ruler can save and conserve the life and being of some of his more noble vassals with the loss of and damage to others less noble, and thus can he procure the increase, prosperity and enrichment of the Spaniards at the cost of the Indians, even though it be with damage and loss to them, as is done in these repartimientos.

The Franciscans answer this objection by falling back on the principle of law that the head of state can secure the good of some at the expense of others, only when so doing is most necessary and important for the *common good.* If this is not true, then it is a well known rule of law that he cannot. The minor of this legal syllogism is "but the repartimientos do not redound to the common good." And the bulk of the answer proves this premise.

Whatever is for the common good of the Indies must be for the common good of both Spaniards and Indians. Actually, it must be more for the good of the Indians than for that of the Spaniards, for the Indians were the original inhabitants of the land, the Spaniards being the strangers and invaders. Therefore the first obligation of the rulers of the land is to secure the spiritual and temporal good of the Indians. But it is obvious that the repartimientos are not for the good of the Indians, "for no proof is necessary than what the eye can see, and the force and violence with which they are taken from their houses and work at the service of the Spaniards, little less than if they were slaves."

Nor are the repartimientos for the spiritual good of the Indians, rather they cause the most grievous type of spiritual harm. Their religious life and formation has been frequently impeded, because, locked in the houses and ranches of the Spaniards, they cannot go to Mass on Sundays and feasts. And though the repartimientos are profitable to the Spaniards from the financial or business point of view, yet they bring spiritual harm even to the Spaniards who attempt to gain a living and to enrich themselves "at such a great spiritual and temporal cost to these poor people."

The author sums up:

And the ruler cannot, with harm to some, procure the good of others, even though it have some appearance or title of common good, when that same good can be had without harm to others. And it is most apparent that the Spanish can maintain themselves in these lands without these repartimientos, just as all other nations and peoples of the world maintain themselves, and I believe it certain that these repartimientos were an invention of Satan to bring many to hell.

SECOND OBJECTION

The second objection is based on a sort of "master race" theory, i.e., that there are some who by their natural superiority, deserve and merit the services which they receive from inferiors. This is all part of the Divine Plan, the divinely established hierarchy of perfection in the world.

God wills that lesser things, and those which are less noble, should serve the greater and nobler, and it is a divine ordinance, especially after [original] sin, that some men should serve others, which is the very thing that Aristotle says in the first book of *Politics,* that there are some men who, because they are by nature superior and prudent, are apt and suitable for ruling and commanding, and others, because they are strong in body and inferior and of less natural wit, ought to be ruled by their betters, and that it is a just thing that the Indians, being inferior, should serve the Spaniards.

The Franciscans answer by distinguishing with Aristotle two types of rule. The first is despotic, which is the relationship existing between master and servant. The other is political (or royal), which has as its object free men, who are not subjected to the will of the ruler in everything. This is the rule of princes and kings, who must rule their subjects for their own good and according to law, not according to whim. The Indians are not under the despotic rule of the Spaniards because they are not slaves; they have been declared free men by Pope Paul III in 1537.

The Indians, therefore, are subject to the second type of rule only. Hence the governors and rulers must look upon them as subjects, as free vassals, and they should rule them for their own good, not for the personal profit of the rulers.

This second type of servitude was found even in the Indians' pre-Columban society and is the natural result of inequalities among men. But the Indians are not by nature servile and even before the coming of the Spaniards their government was sufficient. Here we find echoes of the common ecclesiastical contention that only the gift of faith really justified the Spanish conquest of the New World "for the Indians are a free people, and outside of what concerns the Faith, they were ruled well enough and governed well enough by those among them who were the most prudent and better fitted."

And in what ways were the Indians fit to rule themselves?

With regard to the (type of) rule that is called monastic — which consists of a man himself knowing how to rule himself — and with regard to this the Indians had enough prudence. They also had sufficient economic prudence, which consists in governing one's family. The major rulers also had regnative prudence, which consists of governing a town, province or kingdom. And in the inferiors, (there was also) political (prudence) which consists of knowing how to obey those who command.

Consequently, regarding everything that did not concern their Christian religion, the Indians had no need of the Spaniards nor of Spanish rulers. For the faith, all that they needed were preachers and learned and holy ministers, "because in this regard the Spaniards do them more harm than good with their bad examples and habits."

But another implicit objection immediately presents itself. How can they be fitted to rule themselves since they are habitual drunkards? The answer is that they are not all lazy louts given to drink and that even if they were, this would not necessarily hinder their producing men of greater genius. "And the French, Flemings and Germans sin much by this vice, but they do not therefore cease to be considered peoples of culture." And here the author damns the Spaniards with faint praise. "Although the Spaniards sin little by this vice either because they are more sober or because they have better heads, there are nonetheless infinite numbers of them drunk with other much more dangerous intoxicants, which intoxicate them much more than wine and which blind their understandings 'circa cognitionem et amorem eorum, quae spectant ad salutem aeternam' (Is. 28)." This drunkenness is produced by greed, which as Saint Paul says, is the root of all evil. Greed for honor, for pleasures of the flesh, anger, pride, all these things blind men. Look at the examples of Lucifer, Herod, Absalom, Solomon, Judas and the Pharisees. The Spaniards are literally looking at the mote in the neighbor's eye and ignoring the beam in their own.

THIRD OBJECTION

The third objection is simply the fear of the Spaniards that if the repartimientos are taken away, then the entire country is in danger of perishing, either through hunger or war. This strikes the authors of the memorial as peculiarly ironic, because the Spaniards have no fear of offending God with their eternal vexations and ill-deeds toward the native population. They do not fear the anger of God, they fear only that if they live like Christians and treat the Indians as they ought, that the entire commonwealth will be lost. What nations have ever perished for doing what was right? But, we are told, innumerable ones have perished for failing to do so. We are subjected to a catalogue of faithless nations, including the Assyrians, Chaldeans, Medes, Persians, Greeks, Romans, Egyptians, Chanaanites, Ammorites, Jebusites, Pherezites, Hebrews, Trojans, Thebans and lastly, even the Spaniards themselves (under their Gothic Kings), whom God punished by allowing the infidel Moor to over-

run their land. More recent examples are to be found in Germany, France, Flanders, Bohemia, England and other places.

FOURTH OBJECTION

The repartimientos have taken such root in the land and the Spaniards have had them for so long that now they possess them by prescription. What is referred to here is the *praescriptio longi temporis* of Roman Law, whereby dominion could be obtained, without right or title, by peaceful, good-faith possession over a specified period of time. It was the equivalent of easement or adverse possession in modern American Law. The Spaniards claim that the repartimiento is an immemorial custom, of which they have enjoyed peaceful possession in good faith since the time of the conquest. Consequently it now belongs to them by right and to deprive them of it is unjust.

The objection is answered briefly and legalistically. Even though the repartimientos are of great antiquity, "I answer that sin also is a very old thing in the world, and for this reason it is not good, rather for that very reason it is all the worse." With regard to the Spaniards, they have always been possessors in bad faith, since "everyone has cried out against these repartimientos." A possessor in bad faith has no right of prescription. Also the repartimientos infringe on the liberty of the Indians and against liberty there can be no prescription.

FIFTH OBJECTION

Since these repartimientos are so deeply rooted among the Spaniards, they cannot be removed without great pain and distress on the part of these same Spaniards, some like a "tooth which, because it is so deeply rooted, cannot be extracted without much pain."

The author takes up the answer to this objection directly from the simile used by the objectors.

To this I answer that a decayed tooth is extracted, even though not without much pain in order to avoid the continuous pain that it causes and in order that it will not harm the other teeth; and so it is proper to remove the repartimientos, which cause so much spiritual and temporal harm to the poor Indians. And it does no small harm to the souls of the Spaniards to keep these poor Indians, who are free, so oppressed.

And no matter how much they would like to hide it, the pain of the "decayed tooth" will continue to plague them. And if it does not cause them "dolor grande y escrupulo," so much the worse for a people that professes Christianity.

What are the Spaniards to do? First, they must pacify their own consciences. "Therefore the Spaniards will have to try to put themselves in a good and secure state, and let them not spend their whole lives in a state so dangerous, so harmful and so offensive to so many of their neighbors." Christ himself said that if one's eye is the occasion of sin (escandalizare), it should be plucked out and cast away (Matt. 18). This means that anything, no matter how attached one may be to it, must be avoided if it is the occasion of sin, and especially if it works to the scandal of the neighbor or to the weak. "And what people has there ever been in the world weaker (mas pusilla) than these Indians, to whose scandal and harm the Spaniards have paid and do commonly pay so little attention? And as if that sovereign God were not watching the vexations and calumnies that they commit against these poor creatures."

SIXTH OBJECTION

This objection is based on the necessity of preserving peace and concord among the different races. It is bolstered principally by an appeal to the policy of the primitive Church. Here the Church had to make certain accommodations so that the Jewish and Gentile converts could live in peace with one another. For example, the famous "Council" of Jerusalem decreed that newly-converted Gentiles in the Near East should abstain from blood, things strangled and offered to idols, and from fornication (Acts 15). Again Saint Paul circumcised Timothy, whose mother was a Jew, and he also entered the temple with certain Jews in order to fulfill his Nazarite vow (Acts 21).

The moral, then, is this:

Since if all the aforementioned things were ordained in this way for a short time in order that there should be peace and concord among those converted from Judaism and the Gentiles and in order to remove scandal from the weak Jews (as was seen), it follows that taking away the repartimientos is not the right course, because taking them away would be the occasion of much scandal to the Spaniards, and an act very destructive of peace and union among these peoples.

There is, of course, as the author points out, a vast difference between the two cases. The four Noetic prohibitions mentioned in Acts were most just, for the reasons already mentioned, and quite easy for newly converted Gentiles to follow. Furthermore, no harm, in either the temporal or spiritual order, followed from their observance. Consequently, the whole thing was quite licit as a means of avoiding scandal. But the case of the Indians is entirely different. For the repartimientos are *per se* evil and are opposed to every law, human and divine. Further, they bring about the spiritual and temporal harm of the natives. "And it is a most unjust thing that the Spaniards should seek their peace, repose and contentment at the price of such great harm and loss to the poor Indians, nor is it a just thing that those who govern these Indies should want to remove the unjust scandal of the Spaniards, [thereby] causing most grave scandal among the Indians."

SEVENTH OBJECTION

This is based on a principle of moral theology that it is sometimes better not to disabuse a person who is committing sin through ignorance, lest he then begin to commit it through malice, and without the excusing factor of ignorance.

It is possible that there are some Spaniards who consider the repartimientos licit and this by reason of ignorance and insufficient knowledge, because they are commanded by the commonwealth. And the situation being thus, it seems that since they are in good faith and in ignorance, which is able to excuse from sin, that it would be better to leave them in it and not to take away the repartimientos, in accordance with what the doctors teach . . . of the confessor who finds that his penitent is in sin through ignorance, that sometimes it will be better not to disabuse him, because perhaps once instructed, he will not want to lay [it] aside, and because the ignorance does excuse him.

The author answers this by the classic moral distinction of ignorance which was taught by Saint Thomas (Suma Theol. 12, q. 76, ar. 2). There are, of course, two types of ignorance, invincible and vincible. The former is that ignorance which cannot be easily overcome, or which it is morally impossible to overcome, so that it does excuse from sin, nor is there any obligation to remove one's self from the state (since individuals are not held to the impossible). Vincible ignorance is that which can be overcome. Consequently, since it is a state that a person can remove himself from, it does not per se excuse from sin. The problem at hand is whether the Spaniards' ignorance about the justice of the repartimientos is invincible or vincible. There can be invincible ignorance about divine or human *positive* laws, those which to a great extent depend on the free will of the lawmaker. The natural law is another question. "Because so great is the clarity and refulgence of the natural law, that God planted in the understanding of all men, that it is impossible that a man who has the use of reason (no matter how barbarous or bestial or little less than a brute he may be) should not understand without a preacher or any teacher, the truth and justice of those precepts . . ." Among these natural precepts is the golden rule of "do unto others . . ."

From all this it follows that the Spaniards, who do not want to be treated like slaves, must from the force of the natural law not do the same to the Indians. Consequently there can be no invincible ignorance in what they do.

Nor can they excuse themselves on the grounds that these things have been commanded by the commonwealth or the government, because the civil government cannot give authority to do what is against the natural or divine law. And since there is no question here of producing greater good or avoiding evil, there is no possible excuse and the Spaniards are merely blinding their consciences.

This objection ends with a strange parallel between the Spaniards in Mexico and the Israelites in Egypt. After the manner of an Old Testament Prophet, the author hurls, in somewhat tortured syntax, the threat of divine vengeance against the Spaniards.

It is a strange thing and one much to be pondered, that which is written in Exodus of Pharaoh, King of Egypt, and of his vassals, that when God our Lord had on different occasions sent a command by Moses and Aaron that they should allow to leave their kingdoms the Children of Israel, whom for many years they had held in tyrannical bondage while treating them most unjustly, as the Spaniards do to the Indians . . . when God had many times commanded the Egyptians to let the people of Israel leave their kingdom, and for this reason had sent on them many plagues and frightful scourges, by force of which they finally let them leave Egypt, the Israelites were scarcely departed when Pharao, and his vassals, having repented of the permission they had given, gathered their chariots and armies to follow them and bring them back to Egypt. . . To the letter, this is happening among the Spaniards, who in order not to lose temporal profits which accrue to them from the service of the Indians, turn their faces from such laws as there are, human and divine, and they do not look at the most grave offense that they commit in this matter against God and their neighbor, treating them as if they were their slaves, while they are free, nor does any other thing come before them except whether "we will lose great profit if these repartimientos and services are taken from us."

EIGHTH OBJECTION

This is an argument based on probabilism. It contends that there are many men in the Indies, and many of these are learned and wise men, who hold that the repartimientos are licit. And because these learned men do hold this opinion, it can be called probable "from which it follows that those who govern this kingdom and the rest of the Spaniards can follow it, as with a probable opinion, for the purpose of not removing the repartimientos."

The author answers with a classic moral distinction of intrinsic and extrinsic authority. In all moral discussions of probabilism, intrinsic authority refers to the reasons and moral arguments which bolster the probability of a particular opinion. They are called intrinsic because they follow from the very nature of the opinion itself. On the other hand, extrinsic authority is used to denote the prestige and learning of the various men who hold a particular opinion. Thus, without any consideration of the reasons which bolster a particular opinion, it can be said to have authority precisely because of the prudence, intelligence and good judgment of the men who hold it. Obviously, of the two, intrinsic authority is vastly superior, not only because it is intellectually better, but because it obviates the danger of being led astray by a blind authoritarianism.

This is precisely the point the memorial drives at. Even learned men can err. The obligation of the individual is always to try to find the truth. "Where there are different opinions, I am obliged to follow that which would seem to me to be more probable and to have better foundations and consequently to have a greater demonstration of truth."

The question then is to test the quality (and hence the probability) of the proposition: the repartimientos are licit and should not be abolished.

The answer is that the Devil is history's greatest sophist and one of its most persuasive dialecticians. With sophistic and specious reasoning, he can lead many persons astray, even to the destruction of the Indies

and thus of the souls of the Spaniards. And these latter, "in order to justify their cause, also have their lettered men, their texts and their laws, and it is the permission of God that these who do not wish to hear truths contrary to their appetites, are such as spoke through Isaias, 'speak to us pleasing things, show our errors to us' and those of whom Saint Paul speaks:

For there will come a time when they will not endure the sound doctrine; but having itching ears, will heap up to themselves teachers according to their own lusts, and they will turn away their hearing from the truth and turn aside rather to fables. (2 Timothy 4:3–5)

The Spaniards are doing just what Saint Paul predicted by going about in search of doctors and teachers who will tell them what they want to hear. "They consult one or two or many teachers, and if those tell them the truth which they do not like, they do not stop until they find some one or some ones to tell them what they want." And infinite numbers of Spaniards have practiced the fine art of self-deception by hunting for theologians and teachers who will tell them, not what is just and unjust, but who will justify their particular position. This is not the use of probabilism but "coaceruar y amo[n]tanar maestros, y andar de vno en otro, hasta que halle[n] alguno o algunos, que les hablen, como ellos quiere[n]."

Why are these teachers so wrong and so like the prophets condemned by Isaias, those who went about comforting the people and crying "Peace, peace, and there shall be no peace." Why is their extrinsic authority worthless? It is because it is always easy to find false and specious reasons for the repartimientos, while neglecting the weightiest and most obvious commands of the Divine Law, especially that of charity. For charity "is the love of God and of the neighbor, which consists in not offending nor in stealing what is another's, and in doing for him all possible good . . ." And the opinion which condemns the repartimientos ("if it can be called an opinion and not a most clear truth") is the one most conformable to Divine and human law, natural reason, charity to God and the neighbor, piety and mercy, justice and the rest of the virtues. Hence it is much more probable and worthy of reception and practice, while the contrary is detestable and evil, destructive of the Indies, deceitful, false and contrary to all law, human and divine."

Having disposed of the first doubt and all possible reasons for and objections to the abolition of the repartimientos, the memorial now proceeds to the rest of the doubts proposed by the Council. These answers are quite brief, for, obviously, the matter has been well taken care of in the previous paragraphs.

SECOND DOUBT

Everything that has been said already has taken care of the first doubt and it should suffice for the second also. The various abuses mentioned are all forms of private gain and at the expense of the work and sweat of the Indians. Hence they are never lawful.

THIRD DOUBT

Nor can the repartidores use the Indians in any species of industry, even if the Viceroy or governor gives permission. For the inferior can give no permission contrary to the will or law of the superior, in this case, God, because such permissions are to the notable harm and detriment of the neighbor. The author considers the office of repartidor very dangerous to the salvation of those who hold it, because of the ill-use they make of the freedom they have in allotting Indians.

FOURTH DOUBT

In the fourth doubt, as framed by the Council, reasons are given pro and con vis-a-vis the allotment of Indians to the mines. It is the negative reasons which are definitely better, and which are sufficient to condemn this form of repartimiento. This together with all the things already mentioned should be sufficient.

The rest of the answers have nothing to do with the repartimientos.

THE EVOLVING LABOR SYSTEM

SILVIO ZAVALA

Silvio Zavala (1909–   ) is one of the outstanding interpreters of the colonial period among Mexican historians. He has been more interested in the institutional history than in the political story, and the questions of Indian-Spanish relationships as they translated themselves into the labor problem have been the subject of much of his excellent and enlightening research and writing. He has been a delegate to UNESCO and has served on the staff of El Colegio Nacional, Mexico City. He has been visiting professor and has lectured in a number of American universities, and has been chairman of several major cooperative projects undertaken by historians from all areas of the Western Hemisphere, such as the "Programa de Historia de América," carried on by the Comisión de Historia (which he heads) of the Instituto Panamericano de Geografía e Historia.

Zavala's *La encomienda indiana* is one of the classics in the field of Indian labor studies. The piece here reproduced has been chosen for the light which it sheds on developing labor patterns in the period following the sixteenth-century years of controversy; it is from a series of lectures given some years ago.

UNTIL the middle of the sixteenth century the labor system in New Spain rested upon slaves, who were employed mainly in the mines and at other hard tasks, and upon the personal service rendered on the encomiendas by way of tribute. Both forms represented a system of unpaid labor. Naturally, no wages need be paid to slaves. As for the services rendered to the encomenderos in that early period, these were based upon the theory that the Indians in their encomiendas owed them tribute as vassals, and the personal service that they performed was regarded as a part of their tribute. Consequently, these were likewise a type of unremunerated labor.

The problem of native labor was completely changed when about the middle of the sixteenth century the slaves were freed and, in accordance with the cedula of February 22, 1549, personal service under the encomienda system was prohibited and the encomenderos were henceforth permitted to collect tribute only in kind or in money. It fell to Viceroy Luis de Velasco to struggle with the serious problem raised by this great change in the institutions that had provided the labor supply of New Spain since the beginning of the Conquest. Through what channel would the labor necessary for carrying on the work of the colony now be obtained? Would it be possible to establish a system of voluntary wage labor like that in use in Spain?

Hardly thirty years had passed since the conquest of Mexico brought two completely different civilizations into contact with each other — the European civilization of the sixteenth century and the Indian civilization of the period of Montezuma. It was

From Silvio Zavala, *New Viewpoints on the Spanish Colonization of America* (Philadelphia, 1943), pp. 93–103. Reprinted by permission of the University of Pennsylvania Press.

therefore easy to foresee that the European system of voluntary wage labor would not function satisfactorily as a means of regulating all labor relations between the two groups. Nevertheless, in the instructions of April 16, 1550, the Crown charged Viceroy Velasco to attempt to persuade the Indians to hire out for labor in the cities and the country so that they might not be idle. The enforcement of this order was to be in the hands of the royal authorities in the colony; private Spaniards would have no power to compel the Indians to work even if the Indians belonged to their encomiendas. The Viceroy was to require that their wages be paid to the Indian laborers themselves and not to their chiefs or to any other person. The labor was to be moderate, and those who exacted excessive labor were to be severely punished.

The aim, therefore, was to establish a system of voluntary wage labor with moderate tasks; but in anticipation that the Indians might not offer their services voluntarily, the order further directed the royal authorities in the colony to deliver laborers to colonists who needed them. From one point of view this order was designed to prevent abuses arising from a direct relationship between the Spanish master and the Indian laborer, as shown by the clause forbidding the encomenderos to compel the Indians to work. From another point of view, however, its significance lies in the fact that if the effort to establish a voluntary system of labor should fail through the Indian's refusal to accept work, the state was ready to act as a mediator and to protect the public interest by compelling the laborer to work.

As the economic needs of the European group, accustomed to the agricultural, commercial, and industrial life of sixteenth-century Europe, were greater than those of the Indians, it was certain that there would always be a great demand for labor. On the other hand, as the Indians did not have the same interest in this more highly developed economic life and as their inherited techniques were not the same as those of

the laboring classes of Europe, there was inevitably a perpetual maladjustment between the labor supply and the needs of colonial society.

To all this can be added the incompatibilities of language and religion and the other social and cultural differences between the two great nuclear groups which made up Mexican society. All this explains why the Crown's hopes of shifting immediately from slavery and tribute in personal service to voluntary wage labor were not realized. Outlines of a compromise system — one in which labor was enforced by the governors but was remunerated by wages — began to take shape even during the administration of Viceroy Velasco. Under this system the justices or *jueces repartidores* summoned the Indian workers and assigned them to labor on farms, in mines, on public works, and in the domestic service of colonial society.

This was the origin of what was called in New Spain the *cuatequil* or system of forced wage labor. This system, combined with previous indigenous customs, was to develop on a much larger scale in Peru under the name of *mita,* an institution distinct from both slavery and the personal service of the encomienda, both of which were displaced in the process that we are describing. The advantage to the Indian of this new form of labor as compared with the previous system was that he received a daily wage and that public authorities moderated the hours and the character of his labor. On the other hand, coercion could not be abandoned although voluntary labor was gradually beginning to make its appearance in certain types of work.

The principle advanced by Spanish jurists to justify coercive intervention of the authorities in labor relations rested upon a concept of public interest. They maintained that without Indian labor colonial life could not develop, and that the state could not compromise with general idleness. But the interpretation of public interest given by these writers and by the laws was not confined to public works, but also included, as contributory to the general welfare, the farms, mines, buildings, and other private enterprises of the colonists.

The main differences between the cuatequil of New Spain and the mita of Peru lay in the fact that the former usually affected Indians in districts near the place of work, while in Peru the laborers had to travel much greater distances. In New Spain the work period was almost always one week and each Indian presented himself for work three or four weeks a year. The Peruvian periods of labor lasted for months. The quota of workers raised by the villages of New Spain was commonly 4 per cent, and in Peru one-seventh, or about 14 per cent. In Tucumán one Indian was taken out of every twelve.

The list of people eligible to obtain labor in this way usually included the clergy, the Spanish authorities, and the Indian chieftains, in addition to the Spanish colonists. In the distribution of workers even the lands of the University of Mexico were given preference to other farms

in order that natives who dedicate themselves to study may be encouraged and strengthened to carry on their work and also in order to aid the sons and conquistadors of this New Spain who wish to apply themselves to the study of their choice, whereby it is well known they can gain much honor and profit.

With regard to mining in New Spain, there was a restriction which forbade the use of these Indian laborers, or *tapisques* as they were called, in the interior of the mines. They were employed mainly in the smelting of metals in the mills. The other work was done by the *laboríos*, or voluntary Indian laborers, who usually earned good wages and were given a share of the metal they obtained, and who came to specialize in mining labor.

The extension and consolidation of the system of compulsory wage labor characterized the period covering the administrations of Velasco (1550–1564), Martín Enríquez (1575–1580), and other viceroys up to the beginning of the seventeenth century. In the end it became the chief source of labor in the colony. Not even the encomenderos succeeded in remaining independent of the institution of the cuatequil. If they needed laborers, they could no longer take them directly from their villages as they had formerly done as a form of tribute. Like other private colonists, they were forced to apply to a justice or a juez repartidor for the number of Indians needed, and the workers thus provided no longer worked gratuitously but were entitled to customary wages from the encomendero.

The Indians of the encomienda villages were, moreover, subject to the obligations of this general system of compulsory labor, so that if the authorities in charge thought it advisable to turn them over to someone other than the encomendero, the latter had no right to contest or impede such assignment.

In the preceding chapter we noted that the encomienda carried with it no title to the soil, and we now see that the encomendero lost control over the labor of his Indians since this was regulated independently by the royal authorities.

In the period between 1575 and 1600 an important increase in the wages of the Indians took place. In the beginning they had been paid half a real a day; later, common laborers were paid a real and artisans two reales. The latter were the masons, carpenters, smiths, or other men who knew a trade. The pay was subsequently increased to a real a day and board for the unskilled worker, or one and a half reales. Thus, the amount of the daily wage was tripled.

The liberal ideas which were already active on behalf of the Indians in the middle of the sixteenth century, when they were freed from slavery and from personal service to the encomendero, resulted in a new agitation against the system of compulsory labor. Writers of this persuasion asked themselves if this system was compatible with the free status of the Indians, notwithstanding the reasons of state and public interest advanced in its justification which had already given rise to laws on vagrancy in the European countries.

This movement succeeded in modifying the legislation on the subject, for in 1601 and 1609 new cedulas were issued for the purpose of establishing voluntary, and of putting an end to compulsory, labor for wages. The jueces repartidores were replaced by *comisarios de alquileres,* who were to watch over labor relations but who could not deliver Indians to employers without first consulting the wishes of the laborers. The Indian could now go to the public squares to hire out to whomever he wished, and the only requirement was that he might not remain idle. The Crown expressly stated that its wish was that the natives might live in complete liberty as its vassals, in the same way as its other vassals in the Indies and in Spain.

The colonial authorities, fearing the effects that this change might produce in American economic life, did not enforce the laws with any rigor; in fact, compulsory labor continued. In 1632, however, the Crown repeated the prohibition during the administration of Viceroy Cerrato in New Spain and finally brought about the suspension of all assignments of compulsory labor except in the case of mines.

The effects of the new measure upon agricultural labor were not serious because for years past the Spanish farmers had begun to attract to their farms the Indians of the neighboring villages who were known as *gañanes* or *laboríos.* Thus, instead of waiting for the periodic assignment of Indians by the public authorities, they had Indian families continuously in residence on their own lands as laborers. This provoked conflicts between the Spanish farmers and the Indian villages, for the latter resented the diminution of the number of their people available for compulsory service before this was abolished and the corresponding increase in the amount of work that devolved upon Indians who remained in the village. Consequently the authorities ordered that the gañanes established on the farms of the Spanish colonists should not be exempted from personal service (cuatequil) when their turn came; but it was also permitted that at such times their own employers could retain their services, which would then be debited against the total amount of forced labor to which the employers were entitled as farmers. Hence, when compulsory farm labor was abolished by Cerrato in 1633, the owners of farms already had other sources of labor supply. Moreover, the landowners had begun to do everything in their power to strengthen their hold on their gañanes by depriving them of freedom to leave the farm at will. The legal means of accomplishing this purpose was found in advances of money and goods, which bound the gañán to the land by placing him in debt. This method, and not the old encomienda of the sixteenth century, constitutes the true precursor of the Mexican hacienda of more recent times. Under the latter system the master is the owner of the land through grant, purchase, or other legal title, or perhaps only as a squatter, and he attracts the gañanes to his lands and then keeps them there by means of debts.

Liberal thought in the period of colonization did not fail to look with mistrust upon this system of agrarian servitude through debt, and it denounced the system as formerly it had denounced slavery, the encomienda, and the cuatequil. The Spanish government made significant provisions for limiting the amount of legal indebtedness. For example, at one time it permitted the advance of not more than three months' wages to the rural workers. Again, it limited the sum that could be advanced; this was not to exceed five pesos, and the landowner would lose whatever he advanced above this amount, for no right to collect it was recognized.

Some measures were taken to assure that the wishes of the Indian should be respected if, in spite of his debt, he should desire to move to another estate. Generally the new master paid the debt to the former landowner, and by this means an Indian with well-founded complaints could change residence. On the other hand, the first master was protected when his worker left him without cause and without paying his debts to make an agreement with another landowner.

In spite of all these legal restrictions, an examination of the legal character of the Mexican rural system in the eighteenth century reveals that the farmers had succeeded in extending the system of gañanía and had secured it by means of debt. There were even some cases involving estates with a large population in which, after the royal treasury collected from the owners or their stewards the tribute due from the gañanes to the King, the owner added this debt to those arising from his own advances of money and of goods and used the aggregate debt to bind the worker to his estate.

The growing number of peons and the isolation of estates gave rise gradually to the custom of punishment of the peons by the master or his representatives; but this does not mean that the latter possessed judicial authority, for the King's justice intervened whenever a serious crime was committed.

The system of peonage thus had colonial roots, but in that period the vigilance of the public authorities afforded a measure of protection to the laborers. When, subsequently, laissez faire or other abstentionist theories of public law left the peons alone and defenseless against the economic power of their masters, the harshness of the hacienda regimen increased, and the population and importance of the Indian villages steadily diminished in comparison with the estates employing peons.

We have already said that compulsory labor in mines persisted beyond the year 1633, but that the number of free workers attracted by the relatively high wages of miners increased. The public authorities artificially stimulated this trend when they exempted mine workers (laboríos) from the payment of tribute. It should be noted that it was greatly to the interest of the mine operators to have a regular corps of skilled and diligent Indians for mining work, since the gangs of forced labor assigned to them by the authorities were composed of Indians who knew little about mining and the continual weekly shifting of these gangs interfered with the normal course of operations. Moreover, as we have already remarked, these tapisques could not be legally employed in the underground labor of the mines. Consequently, the mine operators themselves were determined that there should be free, wage-earning labor residing on the properties.

The device of juggled indebtedness functioned in the mines as well as on the haciendas, and foremen sometimes traveled great distances to recover fugitive laborers. Legally, advances of pay could not amount to more than eight months' wages. Many conflicts were caused by the practice followed by some employers of enticing Indians away from others by offering them more money or better working conditions. Legislative policy was always opposed to this practice because it left the first operator without labor and with unpaid Indian debts.

The consummation of the process of replacing the forced laborer (tapisque) by the free laborer for wages (laborío) was witnessed by Alexander von Humboldt when he visited New Spain at the beginning of the nineteenth century. It was for this reason that he wrote that the work in the Mexican mines was performed by free labor.

Sugar mills presented serious labor problems. The government very soon imposed limitations upon the use of forced Indian labor in these mills; and, in line with its restrictive policy, it even went so far as to forbid the construction of new mills. Land could not be devoted to the planting of sugar cane without a previous certification that such land was unsuitable for the planting of corn or wheat, and only in such case was the planting of sugar cane permitted.

The official explanation of the restriction of Indian labor in the mills was the harm suffered by natives performing that type of work. The evidence shows that economic as well as humanitarian considerations were involved. The Crown recommended that millowners buy Negroes to take the place of the Indians and even forbade the Indians to hire out voluntarily for such labor.

The industry of cloth mills also was important. These consumed the wool produced on the large sheep ranches manufacturing certain fabrics that were sold in domestic trade. In spite of copious legislation favoring free labor in these infant industries, the work in them was in fact a rigorous form of servitude. The laborers lived a life of close confinement, like those who worked in bakeries and tanneries. Generally they were bound by a system of indebtedness, although some of them were convicts. The criminal branch of the Audiencia of Mexico was empowered to sell convicted felons into service in the cloth mills, and the sentences could run for several years. Humboldt professed to be particularly distressed by the working conditions that he observed in this industry.

Among the workers in the cloth mills were many Chinese who came from the Philippines by way of Acapulco. The slave traffic in Orientals came to have a certain importance in New Spain, although in the seventeenth century they were ordered to be set free. Perhaps the presence of these laborers explains some of the influences noted in the style of Mexican fabrics.

The improvement of labor conditions in the cloth mills was not the only concern of the Crown in this matter. In accordance with the mercantilist policy, which tended to favor manufacturing in the mother country at the expense of that in the colonies, it imposed a series of restrictions on the types of fabrics whose manufacture was permitted in colonial mills and on their sale. Likewise, a close watch was kept over the erection of new establishments.

In summary, in the face of many obstacles the system of colonial labor progressed from slavery, from unpaid personal services in lieu of tribute, from forced labor, and from debt peonage, toward a standard of free paid labor, that is, toward the economy common to the modern world.

As a rule, the colonial stage of Hispanic-American history has been thought of as one characterized by great tranquillity and by a minimum of problems. This idea, however, is perhaps due to the preference that has been given to political history as understood by the nineteenth century, and to the neglect of social history. For as soon as we fix attention on the tremendous problems of organization and labor presented by the period of colonization, this illusion is at once dispelled; and in its place we see a spectacle of constant change in the basic structure of the labor system — a social phenomenon manifestly of exceeding interest.

A CASE STUDY: THE AZTECS UNDER THE
SPANISH LABOR SYSTEMS

CHARLES GIBSON

Charles Gibson (1930–) took his undergraduate work at Yale; he did graduate work at the University of Texas and was doctorated at Yale in 1950. He is currently professor at the University of Michigan, having moved there from the State University of Iowa to fill the chair long held by the eminent Latin Americanist Irving Leonard, recently retired. Professor Gibson has held both Guggenheim and Rockefeller Foundation fellowships; during the year 1956–57 he was visiting professor at Harvard. From 1955 to 1960 he served as associate managing editor of the *Hispanic American Historical Review*. Among Latin American historians Professor Gibson is a colonialist. Two of his earlier studies were *The Inca Concept of Sovereignty and the Spanish Administration in Peru* and *Tlaxcala in the Sixteenth Century*.

The following selection is from Gibson's latest, most thorough, and enlightening study. It was chosen to show a case study of the Spanish labor systems in action.

In Aztec society, labor had been prescribed and carefully regulated. Agricultural labor was a primary responsibility of maceguales in the system of common landholding. Labor in the towns or in the town subdivisions, as for the construction or repair of community buildings, was required of the able-bodied inhabitants of all cabeceras and sujetos. Local Indian rulers depended upon groups of workers to perform communal tasks, with minimal individual assignments. What impressed the Spanish oidor Alonso de Zorita concerning Indian labor in the early sixteenth century was the sense of contribution, the "merriment" and "great rejoicing" that attended it. Beyond this, and in some measure exploiting it, had been the imperial labors of Aztec society, including the military services demanded by Montezuma.

It is evident that native peoples of the conquest period were vulnerable to the Spaniards' demands for labor. Accustomed to providing their own sustenance and to both local and distant service without pay, Indians appeared to be ready to perform, and even to derive satisfaction from, occupations that were monotonous or degrading in European eyes. In Europe, unskilled mass labor carried implications of coercion or enslavement. In the Indian tradition the same mass labor, if not too onerous, might be considered rewarding as a shared and pleasurable experience.

Spaniards quickly took advantage of the Indian attitude toward directed labor. By controlling the tlatoque, Cortés and other Spaniards easily manipulated masses of workers. A major change under Spanish rule, however, was that Indian peoples lost

Reprinted from *The Aztecs under Spanish Rule: A History of the Indians of the Valley of Mexico, 1519–1810* by Charles Gibson, pp. 220–256, with the permission of the publishers, Stanford University Press. © 1964 by the Board of Trustees of the Leland Stanford Junior University.

the sense of joyous participation and adopted an attitude of resignation. From the mid-sixteenth century until the end of the colonial period they acceded to Spanish demands for employment without the ceremonial communality that had attended the pre-conquest and the first post-conquest labor enterprises. Labor tended thus to move from the social, moral, and spiritual categories, in which Indians had placed it, into the economic or physical categories of Europe. The memory of earlier Indian values was retained, however unsympathetically, in Spanish society. As a colonist stated in the seventeenth century, "It is well known that Montezuma gave tasks to Indians with no other purpose than to entertain them."

Spaniards did not need any mass enslavement of Indians in the Valley of Mexico. Slavery was not unknown in the early colonial period, but it derived mainly from Spanish experience with societies of other types. In individual cases it operated under a guise of legitimacy whenever Indians could be shown to be occupying a "slave" status already in Indian society — for this could be understood as a change of masters rather than as an initial enslavement. When Spaniards asked for slaves from upper-class Indians, non-slaves might be delivered instead, for, in the words of Ramírez de Fuenleal, if an Indian ruler called a macegual a slave, "lo era." Moreover, Spanish raiding expeditions introduced Indian captives from outside the Valley, and these also were sold as slaves in the capital in the early years.

But the native institutions of mass labor were more appropriately controlled by encomienda than by slavery, and encomienda proved to be the more important institution. In practice, both slavery and encomienda had a considerable flexibility, for workers under either system could be sold or hired to other employers and utilized in illegal ways. Furthermore, the early relations between Spaniards and Indians brought into being a variety of lesser labor institutions. In the corregimientos of the 1530's and after, labor provisions were specified in tribute regulations. The early church, by persuading and influencing the caciques, employed Indian workers in the construction of ecclesiastical buildings and in other servicios personales. In Tenochtitlan and Tlatelolco the first Spanish tribute exactions consisted almost wholly of demands for labor, with service to the viceroy, the construction of civic buildings, the repair and filling of canals, and other tasks contributing to the maintenance of the colonial capital. Only in mining, because the Valley itself possessed no precious metals, did difficulties arise in the employment of the Valley's laborers.

In labor as in tribute, one effect of encomienda and of other types of early Spanish control was to decentralize the imperial Aztec organization and to place emphasis on the separate town units of cabeceras and sujetos. For a generation after the first labor drafts for the rebuilding of the city, no other single large-scale endeavor required the mobilization of more than local segments of the laboring population. Service to encomenderos and corregidores and the construction of ecclesiastical buildings were town enterprises. The Spanish recipients of Indian labor depended upon town organizations, profiting from the authority of each community's tlatoani, from the many calpulli subdivisions, from the tequitlatos, and from the macegual classes accustomed to orderly direction. In Indian society the labor obligation of a sujeto to its cabecera constituted a fundamental relationship recognized by all, and it was universally turned to Spanish uses.

Spaniards used the term llamamiento to signify the act of summons whereby a tlatoani convoked the laborers of the sujetos for the construction of community houses, common agricultural labor, personal service, or other work. The Nahuatl term, coatequitl, implied in practice a division of tasks among the calpulli subdivisions, in a labor structure wherein each calpulli might be responsible for a different specialty and a given portion of the work. In the service continuously provided by sujetos to their cabeceras, these Indian arrangements still applied. Thus in Xochimilco in the late sixteenth century barrios still recognized their special tasks in coatequitl service. Even in the eighteenth century, when a cabecera's community houses required repair or when local road work was to be done, the provision of materials and the work itself were parceled among the sujetos. But from the beginning the sujeto obligations were extended to include service to Spaniards. For the early Spanish construction labors in Mexico City, the drafts were subdivided by barrios and were governed, in part, by barrio specializations. When the Marqués del Valle ordered Indians of Coyoacan to build the house of the oidor Quesada in 1548, the workers supplied the materials, the labor was organized by sujetos, and each sujeto worked on a designated task. In Quesada's construction 340 Indians were directed to bring seventeen wooden beams, an indication not only of the continuing use of a vigesimal organization, but also of the high ratio of laborers to labor units, with twenty Indians for each beam.

Encomenderos, ecclesiastics, and employers of all sorts relied on *tamemes* (Nahuatl, sing. *tlamama*), or Indian carriers, for the provision of goods and for transport. Human carrying had pre-conquest antecedents — since native society lacked vehicles and beasts of burden — but the early colony greatly expanded its role and its dimensions. Royal orders forbidding human carriers on humanitarian grounds met strenuous opposition and were accordingly modified or revoked. Many types of tameme regulation were attempted — voluntary carrying, licensing, confinement to fixed routes, reduction of the distances to be traversed, limitations on the size or weight of loads — but for the most part in vain. Ultimately certain supply routes, notably those connecting Mexico City with the coasts, were served by animal pack trains in numbers sufficient to absorb the commodity traffic, and the problem was in some degree resolved. But as

late as the early seventeenth century royal orders were still being issued forbidding tamemes, and colonists were still arguing their necessity.

The royal orders are indicative of a more general monarchical attitude with regard to Indian labor. By many means in the sixteenth century the crown sought to create a working force that would be free to choose its own tasks and adequately recompensed in wages. Such a working force never came into being in the colonial period, but royal efforts to implement it contributed to major changes in the relations between employers and workers during the middle years of the sixteenth century and after. As a first step, the crown resolved to eliminate unrecompensed labor from the tribute schedules. The basic order of 1549 and subsequent orders in ensuing years announced this prohibition and proposed as a substitute a rotational system of hire, with moderate labor, short hours, limited distances of travel, and wages. The rules were to apply in both encomienda and corregimiento. They implied that coercion was unnecessary and that Indians would work voluntarily if a sufficient wage were provided.

Officials in New Spain took the royal orders seriously, and tribute regulations in encomienda and corregimiento after the mid-century sharply reduced, although they never fully eradicated, unrecompensed labor. The cabildo of the city denounced the rules and attributed to them the labor shortages of subsequent years. Long afterwards Suárez de Peralta recorded his childhood recollections of the consternation that the mid-century restrictions had created among the affluent white class. "Previously everyone's house was filled with whatever the land provided," he asserted, "but the moment that these rules took effect everything had to be bought, properties began to deteriorate, and people found themselves in need."

It is not surprising that the recipients of the cheap mass labor of the first colonial generation attributed the decline of the working force to royal legislation against encomienda services. But other causes were simultaneously at work to bring about modifications in the conditions of Indian employment during the mid-century years. Whether by accident or design, the labor legislation of 1549 appeared at one of the critical moments in the shifting population ratio of whites and Indians — the period following the plague of 1545–48. Although encomenderos tended to blame the king, it became increasingly evident to the growing class of non-encomenderos that encomienda could not meet the needs of the whole white population. The uneconomical labor institutions of the first colonial years would no longer suffice. After the mid-century there were not enough workers to support such institutions, and many new non-encomendero landowners were making claims upon Indian manpower.

The resolution of these problems was repartimiento. The word means distribution or apportionment, and it was applied to a series of diverse colonial procedures, including encomienda grants, land allotment, tribute apportionment, forced sale, and draft labor. For the moment, we adopt the most common usage of the sixteenth and seventeenth centuries, identifying as repartimiento the institution that dominated the recruitment of Indian workers for a period of about seventy-five years after the mid-century. It was a system of rationed, rotational labor, purportedly in the public interest or for the public utility, affecting both encomienda and non-encomienda Indians, and benefiting a much larger employer class than had been possible under encomienda. In fact, it did not fulfill the royal demands for short hours, moderate tasks, or voluntary labor for wages. But it subjected the labor procedures of the colony to administrative scrutiny for the first time, and it satisfied, at least temporarily, the needs of the new colonial employers.

The origins of repartimiento, as would be expected, antedate 1549. The principles of compulsion and rotation, which were essential to it, had precedents in both pre-conquest and early colonial labor. Communities had alternated in service for Nezahualcoyotl in the fifteenth century, and they alternated in service for the viceroy in the early sixteenth century. It is a remarkable fact that Cortés's earliest encomienda regulations relate closely to procedures later established for repartimiento. In the 1520's Cortés ordered a rotational system for encomienda whereby Indians would work for their encomenderos in shifts of twenty days, with thirty-day intervals between working periods for each laborer. Cortés's rules provided for means of inspection, forbade the involvement of women and children, allowed for overtime pay and sustenance, and limited the daily labor to the period between sunrise and one hour before sunset. Such regulations were never seriously enforced in encomienda. But Cortés's principle of rotation and some of the details of his humanitarian regulation were reactivated in repartimiento, when repartimiento labor became separated from encomienda.

Given these antecedents, it appears entirely natural that the Mexico City flood crisis of 1555 should have been met by a repartimiento organization. This was the first of a long series of inundations and threatened inundations in the colonial history of the city. Exceptionally heavy rains, beginning in mid-September, raised the level of the surrounding lake and damaged the city's streets and causeways. In early November the viceroy summoned a huge labor force of about six thousand Indians. Unofficially, the labor force was estimated at over two million. The work began in early December and continued for about four months. Remedial measures included the closing of the sluice openings of certain causeways, the shifting of the courses of several streams, and especially the construction of the new Albarradón de San Lázaro, a protective dike lying closer to the city than its pre-conquest counterpart and extending from the Guadalupe causeway along the entire eastern edge of the urban zone. The dike was approximately twenty feet wide and over four miles long. Vast supplies of lumber and other materials were required. Labor was organized by enforced rotation, with the Indian workers returning to their homes at the end of a week's work to be replaced by a new shift. The work was of unusual severity, much of it was performed in and under the water, and many workers died.

This repartimiento of 1555–56, created as it was by viceregal order in response to emergency conditions, occupies a significant, but short-lived, role in repartimiento history. The more important, because longer lasting, repartimientos of the middle sixteenth century were those dedicated to urban construction and to agricultural labor on the wheat farms of the area surrounding the city. The new emphasis upon non-encomienda employment in agriculture is readily explained. The capital had become a major Spanish metropolis and market, with a white population of some fifteen hundred or two thousand families and a correspondingly greater demand for foodstuffs. With escheatment and population loss, encomienda had deteriorated as an instrument of agricultural supply. Land grants had been issued to private colonists in many areas, and wheat and cattle farms had become numerous. The privately owned farm was already rivalling encomienda as a supplier of food when suddenly, in 1549, the royal prohibition of labor services in encomienda further limited encomienda's role in agricultural provision. For all these reasons a new agricultural repartimiento was called for and came into being.

Our earliest record of the new agricultural repartimiento is dated July 1550. The date follows so closely the prohibition of labor services in encomienda that an immediate causal relation may be supposed. As one of his last acts in office, and at a time of acute shortages of wheat and maize in the city, Viceroy Mendoza ordered the "caciques y gobernadores, alcaldes y principales" of the area surrounding Mexico City to send workers in specified numbers for the cultivation of wheat plantations. During some five years the repartimiento served officially as a combined draft for the wheat farms and for the Spanish citizens of the city, in house construction and other tasks. When in August 1555, a month before the flood, the urban labor was forbidden (except by Indian residents of Tenochtitlan and Tlatelolco) the fact signified a full viceregal commitment to the agricultural draft. At the same time the official in charge of repartimiento, entitled *repartidor,* was given power to use force, to make arrests, and to sentence culprits to prison. By the early 1560's the repartimiento was officially engaging the labor of approximately 2,400 Indian workers per week, distributed among 114 Spanish agriculturists at an average of about twenty workers per employer.

Throughout the rest of the sixteenth century, agricultural repartimiento was a systematically functioning institution. There was installed in each of three subdivisions of the Valley a *juez repartidor,* who was responsible for the administration of the Indian workers and their distribution to Spanish agriculturists. The jueces repartidores were assisted by tenientes, by Indian alguaciles, and by interpreters. Indians were furnished from the towns of the repartimiento jurisdictions in weekly shifts at fixed quotas and were delivered to those Spanish agricultural employers whose properties were located in the same jurisdictions. The detailed procedure, altered only slightly in the last decades of the sixteenth century, was as follows.

Population records were first collected for every contributing community, and from these a percentage quota, at first approximating two per cent of the tributaries, was computed. Each community was then expected to furnish its assigned number of workers each week. The Indian governments of the towns were provided with written or pictorial records listing the names, sujeto affiliations, and tequitlatos of all Indian laborers. As in tribute, temporary reductions might be permitted in periods of epidemic or of labor on local churches.

Every Monday morning the Indians from the towns of each repartimiento area assembled at a given distribution point. They were dispatched, in time for the Monday arrival, by the Indian officials of their communities and conducted to the repartimiento center by local Indian alguaciles. On Monday morning, inside a corral, the juez repartidor issued to the Spanish farmers (*labradores*) or to their agents the Indians assigned to them, in accordance with the amount of wheat each had under cultivation and the requirements of the fields, a matter that depended upon the judgment of the juez repartidor. At the same time the juez repartidor received from the Spanish employers one cuartillo (one-fourth real) for each Indian granted, and from this sum he paid the local alguaciles one real for each eight Indians delivered. Once each year the juez repartidor collected from the labradores one-half real for each fanega they had sown. The income received from the cuartillos and half reales formed a fund from which he paid a salary of twelve pesos per year to the several alguaciles who assisted him. The remainder he kept to supplement his own salary of 250 pesos. All transactions were duly recorded in the account books of the repartimiento.

On Monday morning each labrador or his agent returned to his farm with the Indians assigned to him. There the Indians worked the fields, commonly under a Negro or some other overseer, for a period of one week, from Tuesday to the following Monday, Sunday being a day of rest. On the afternoon of the second Monday, the Indians received their pay and were released to return to their communities. Their places were immediately taken by a new group, which had been collected, assigned, and delivered in the same manner. Thus the qualified Spanish agriculturists were assured of a steady working force in weekly rotation, the drain upon any contributing community was minimized by the quota system, and no single individual was held liable to

the draft more often than three or four times per year. An Indian laborer's guaranty against excessive summons was a receipt issued to him by the juez repartidor, indicating the number of terms he had served since the beginning of the year.

The local operation of repartimiento, with which Spaniards were rarely concerned, continued to follow the procedures of the indigenous coatequitl. In the sixteenth and early seventeenth centuries Spanish repartimiento and Indian coatequitl existed side by side, influencing each other. In repartimiento as in tribute, Indian governments sought to maintain existing Indian organizations and existing exemptions applying to sub-macegual classes, who remained in the service of local Indian rulers. Occasionally Indians arranged a labor differentiation among barrios by assigning coatequitl to certain sujetos while making others liable to repartimiento. Since the Spanish state did not normally regulate the procedures for the selection of workers, but instead made Indian governments responsible for the delivery of a stated number, repartimiento could, at first, be adapted to the Indian organization of cabeceras, sujetos, and calpultin, wholly or almost wholly under Indian control.

In one other fundamental way labor repartimiento depended upon Indian precedents. We revert here to the pre-conquest imperial labor organization and to the jurisdictions of the aboriginal tribes. The repartimiento subdivisions of the 1550's — the areas of Mexico, Texcoco, Tacuba, Chalco — were original Indian tribal areas, and, as we have observed, the viceroy of 1555 deliberately sought out information on the organization of imperial Aztec labor to provide a model for repartimiento. This reliance on the imperial Indian system pertained to labor but not to tribute, since labor, unlike tribute, had been separated from encomienda in 1549 and centralized under the repartimiento system. Changes affecting the points of distribution were made after 1555, but as late as the 1570's the main Indian jurisdictions of the Acolhuaque, the Tepaneca, and the Chalca were still clearly distinguishable in repartimiento administration.

Later, however, repartimiento jurisdictions underwent continuous modification, and the structural relationship with Indian precedents became obscured. . . .

As the native population declined in the late sixteenth century, and as new stresses were imposed upon the methods of recruitment, other elements of continuity from Indian labor traditions were likewise progressively abandoned. Indian governments compelled women, disabled persons, and skilled workers (oficiales) to pay a charge for exemption, or to hire substitutes in labor obligation. Alcaldes sometimes sought to make principales liable, and the officers of town governments themselves were not always excused. With the decline of sub-macegual classes, principales tended to divert workers from coatequitl and repartimiento to private labor on the principales' own fields. When quotas could no longer be met, the sub-macegual exemptions failed, and the remaining sub-macegual peoples were required to contribute to the drafts. Even tequitlatos, alguaciles, and mandones — the very Indian officials responsible for the delivery of workers — were in some instances declared liable in repartimiento labor.

Spaniards, of course, demanded additional workers, both in farming and in other forms of employment. The non-agricultural repartimientos did not cease with the establishment of the agricultural assignments, but remained as simultaneous competing labor drafts. The viceregal government adopted a lenient policy with regard to Spanish petitions for extraneous Indian laborers, and the systematic labor pools provided by repartimiento were a tempting source from which to derive workers for other purposes. In the northern part of the Valley some towns became subject to the repartimientos for the Pachuca mines. Drafts outside the Valley were permitted to draw workers from the Valley's repartimientos in times of critical need. The de-

mand for workers on various construction jobs in the city could not be met from within the city itself, and repartimiento Indians from Xochimilco, Chalco, Texcoco, Tacuba, and other jurisdictions were used for public works, monasteries, the casas reales, the Cathedral, the streets, or the city's water supply, all in addition to agricultural repartimiento. At times the recipients of agricultural laborers leased them informally to private employers in the city, so that Indians nominally designated for the farms found themselves engaged instead in illegal urban labor for individual Spaniards. A count made by the protesting Spanish employers of Chalco in 1599 enumerated eighty-three repartimiento Indians who were being occupied each week in extra tasks, an annual total of about 4,300 laborers, all from the Chalco repartimiento jurisdiction. In a single year, according to the same report, 5,470 Indians from Chalco had labored on the hospital at Oaxtepec. The customary viceregal response to such protests was to suppress some of the additional drafts, but the problem always recurred, and no over-all policy was ever achieved to resolve the conflicting claims of agricultural and non-agricultural employers.

Further drains upon the manpower of the Valley appeared in the form of the servicio de zacate, the servicio de piedra, and other "servicios" demanded by the viceregal government. These exactions were intermediate between labor and tribute. They required the provision of material goods, but Spaniards in general did not classify them as tribute because the goods were paid for. The requirement that the goods be provided nevertheless constituted a labor demand, and Spaniards referred to the operation as repartimiento. From the earliest days of the colony designated towns had to bring to the city daily canoe loads of fodder, fuel, fish, eggs, chickens, stone, lumber, and other materials for the royal officials and other citizens. The payments for these were lower than the market prices of the goods, and it often happened that gobernadores and principales took all the payment, leaving nothing for the suppliers. . . . The specifications as to quantity and frequency of delivery underwent continuous change. But throughout the sixteenth and early seventeenth centuries a royal official in the capital could expect a regular, preferential, and inexpensive supply of necessary goods — a canoe-load of fodder each day, two loads of firewood per week, and food and service to supply his needs. In time the servicios became less demanding, but they continued through the whole period of agricultural repartimiento.

As would be expected, the decreasing population and the various drains on manpower had consequences for the quotas and the number of workers actually provided. During the first thirty years of agricultural repartimiento, quotas for the growing season continued to approximate two per cent of tributaries. Quotas for other periods of the year approximated one per cent, and the year was equally divided between the *sencilla* (November through April) and the *dobla* (May through October). Actual percentages varied. The largest cabeceras, including Xochimilco, Tlalmanalco, and Tacuba, were required to give one hundred workers per week. For all towns giving over fifteen workers the early quotas were expressed in multiples of ten. Until the plague of 1576 the Indian population was sufficiently large and the number of Spanish employers still sufficiently limited to permit low quotas and rounded numbers in agricultural drafts. But with the depopulation of the late 1570's and after, jueces repartidores, on their own authority, resorted to quotas in excess of two per cent. Viceregal rules of the late sixteenth century authorized quotas of four and five per cent in the sencilla and ten per cent in the dobla, at times varying these percentages depending upon liabilities to other drafts or other special circumstances. Occasionally in the early seventeenth century the viceroy offered options to Indian towns: two per cent in the sencilla and ten per cent in the dobla, or four per cent in the sencilla and

eight per cent in the dobla, or five per cent over the year. But whatever the quota for any individual town, the trend was toward an increase in the required percentages from the 1550's to the early seventeenth century.

In addition the dobla periods changed. Doblas of the 1580's were commonly granted in periods of four, six, eight, or ten weeks, depending on the season and the urgency of the Spaniards' petitions. Two annual dobla periods were granted in the 1590's, one for weeding in July or August, and one for harvest in November or December. In the 1590's grants for eight-week and ten-week doblas became more frequent, and a total annual dobla of sixteen to twenty weeks came to be regarded as normal during the years when the dobla of ten per cent was adopted. In the 1590's, too, this schedule was progressively disrupted by the demands of those labradores who had adopted irrigated wheat, the harvesting of which usually occurred in May or June. At first irrigation was slight, and the extra demand could be accommodated by temporary doblas in selected towns. But by the late 1590's all agricultural repartimiento jurisdictions had to make adjustments for irrigated wheat. This was done principally by anticipating the dobla for designated communities, discounting the regular dobla proportionately, and providing the irrigated fields with sencilla quotas during the regular dobla. In times of special need all workers might be utilized for the irrigated crop. Scheduling difficulties became more serious with the development of partially irrigated wheat fields, which required weeding when the fully irrigated wheat fields were ready for harvest. During the overlapping doblas of the early seventeenth century Indians from the public works (*obras publicas*) in the city were sometimes diverted to farm labor. Meanwhile dobla periods were increased to twenty-four or thirty weeks per year, thus approximating and even exceeding the original six-month periods. And the doblas of ten per cent in the seventeenth century, of course, imposed a far heavier burden upon the contributing communities than the doblas of two per cent in the early years.

The conditions of repartimiento accordingly became more burdensome. Indian communities found themselves progressively harder pressed to supply the workers demanded. As in tribute, the increased pressures brought about an abandonment of traditions, an adoption of new and more coercive measures, and a steady accumulation of arrears. As in tribute, Indian governments were held responsible, and gobernadores who were unable to supply their quotas were threatened with arrest and jail sentences. At the same time the competition among Spaniards for Indian workers became more intense, and the frequency and sophistication of malfeasance increased. Spaniards sequestered laborers, beat them, refused to pay them, seized their food and clothing to prevent their escape, and undertook to acquire private native workers outside the drafts. Jueces repartidores repeatedly sought to procure more Indians than the quotas permitted. The repartimiento system of the late sixteenth century was everywhere one of compulsion and abuse, and it received continuous criticism from the clergy.

The meaning of these developments for the actual delivery of workers is suggested by records of the Chalco repartimiento in the years 1619–20. Surviving documents give the sencilla and dobla quota for each community of the Chalco repartimiento in these years and the numbers in fact delivered week by week. The records demonstrate that the Chalco towns at this time were making no exact differentiation between the sencilla and the dobla, and that they failed to meet their quotas, rarely sent the same number twice in succession, and at times defaulted entirely. The total numbers delivered during successive weeks in these years present a most irregular pattern. The dobla periods for weeding and harvesting were periods of increased provision of workers, but the increases were not uniform

and at no time was the full dobla, 647 workers, ever delivered to the Spanish employers.

In the seventeenth century the evident deficiencies of repartimiento resulted in attempts to reform the entire structure of colonial labor. The initial royal reform order in 1601 forbade compulsion in the recruitment of laborers and ruled that repartimiento was to be terminated in agriculture, building, and all other occupations except mining. Indians were to choose their Spanish employers voluntarily, the office of juez repartidor was to be abolished, and corregidores were to require only that Indians offer themselves in appointed places for hire. It is clear that the royal intention in 1601 was to bring to an end the evils of repartimiento. Yet the orders granted discretion to the viceroy with respect to the jueces repartidores, and the provision that Indian workers were to convene in appointed places under the charge of corregidores could be interpreted as entailing no radical departure. The former jueces repartidores did assume new titles — notably, the title *juez comisario de alquileres*. The repartimientos for public works in Tenochtitlan and Tlatelolco were formally abolished, and the viceroy personally visited the plazas of both communities to ensure that Indians would hire themselves "freely and voluntarily." But all attempts to halt repartimiento permanently by means of such legislation uniformly failed. In the metropolitan plazas, where the viceroy demonstrated a desire for genuine reform, "voluntary" labor became farcical. The financial transaction of repartimiento persisted without appreciable change. Labradores paid the jueces comisarios as they had paid the jueces repartidores for Indian laborers, in consideration of the amount of wheat sown, and the jueces comisarios in turn paid the Indian officers who recruited the workers. Private payments, bribery, and fraud frustrated efforts to reform the system. In agricultural repartimiento even the nominal recognition of jueces comisarios de alquileres was soon abandoned. By 1607 the former title, juez repartidor, was again making its appearance, and in subsequent years the old and new titles were indiscriminately employed. The provision that jueces might compel attendance by force, still in accordance with the system of quotas, rendered the new institution essentially unchanged from the old.

The crown sought again in 1609 to bring repartimiento to an end, this time more gradually, through the exercise of viceregal controls. By degrees after this date new viceregal and audiencia rules did bring about formal abolition. In the 1620's the audiencia forbade certain features of urban repartimiento, and of the remaining servicios. Finally, a viceregal order of 1632 issued the definitive repartimiento prohibition. The termination of all repartimientos, except those in mines, was to take effect January 1, 1633.

In Mexican history significant changes have rarely occurred as a consequence of law. Law provides an approximation of historical happening, or a commentary upon it. In the case of the abolition of 1632 it would be an error to suppose either that repartimiento labor came to an end or that law alone was responsible for the transition to other forms of labor organization. It is true that repartimiento played a negligible role in agricultural labor thereafter. But it is also true that it played a negligible role in the period just prior to the abolition. The deficiencies of the Chalco repartimiento at the beginning of the 1620's were wholly characteristic, and a steady deterioration occurred during the next decade. From 1630 to 1632 the labradores of Tacuba received no Indians in repartimiento. The 130 farms of the Tepozotlan repartimiento received an average of one Indian per month. The labor failure, as is obvious, had little relation to the royal and viceregal prohibitions. Instead, two other factors, originally independent but progressively interrelated in the early seventeenth century, brought about the decline of the agricul-

tural repartimiento. One of these was Desagüe labor. The other was hacienda labor, which was dependent upon private working forces and peonage.

In the history of the Valley of Mexico, the term Desagüe refers to the process by which the lake areas of the conquest period were converted into the salt-dust flats of today. During colonial times labor on the Desagüe was organized manual labor, differing from agricultural labor in the erratic character of its employment and provision. The size of the Desagüe working forces was determined by irregular floods and by the successive states of anxiety experienced by viceregal administrations. In times of emergency available resources were strained to the limit. At other times, and for long periods, the Desagüe was permitted to languish.

Whenever prolonged rains occurred, lake levels rose, flood conditions prevailed, and the low-lying areas became inundated. But Spanish authorities rarely paid attention to floods elsewhere than in the city. Flood danger and Desagüe operations were almost invariably measured in terms of potential damage in the capital. In the early city the streets and plazas were situated at higher levels than the houses, which suffered first from increases in the water level. The chief measure of earlier control had been the pre-conquest dike (*albarradón*), constructed in the late 1440's under Montezuma I and Nezahualcoyotl, and enlarged at the end of the fifteenth century under Ahuitzotl. The most critical sixteenth-century emergency, the inundation of 1555–56, resulted in the construction of the new dike, the Albarradón de San Lázaro.

Spaniards in the sixteenth century, like Indians in the pre-conquest period, favored a system of flood protection by dike. But Spaniards proposed, without ever executing, large-scale remedial measures of other kinds. Initial plans were made in 1555–56 to divert the Río de Cuauhtitlan, and to construct a lengthy drainage canal from Lake Texcoco north to the Río de Tula, a distance of more than twenty miles. Subsequent proposals for the drainage of the waters surrounding the city were advocated in the belief that the urban site would become more healthful and that lands might be reclaimed for use. On the occasion of a minor flood in 1579–80, surveys were made for a drainage operation from Ecatepec to Huehuetoca. Humanitarian criticism of these plans took the position that the heavy labor involved would destroy the Indian workers. The humanitarian opposition did not prevail, but other factors — notably the natural decline of flood waters and the failure to appreciate the magnitude of the problem — operated to forestall any effective action. As a whole, and apart from the years 1555–56, the sixteenth century may be regarded as a period of complacency with regard to water levels.

More serious flooding, accompanied by heavy damage in the city, occurred in 1604 and 1607. It is probable that the city's vulnerability to flood waters had been steadily increasing during the late sixteenth century as a result of the cutting of the surrounding forest and the progressive silting of the lake. City life had also changed in ways that made flood waters far more injurious: canals had been filled, boat traffic had declined, new houses had been built in an assumption of safety, and city ways had become increasingly farther removed from the amphibious living of the late Aztec and early colonial period. With the floods of the early seventeenth century, small causeways and wooden bridges reappeared and canoe traffic revived in the city. The flood of 1607 was more severe than that of 1604, but together they stimulated a program of relief and repair far more ambitious than any undertaken in the sixteenth century. The Albarradón de San Lázaro was now rebuilt; the causeways of Guadalupe, San Cristóbal, and San Antonio Abad were repaired; and work was begun on a dam, the Presa de Acolman, to contain the waters of the Río de Teotihuacan (Nexquipaya). Most important, a new and far larger program of Desagüe General was now inaugu-

rated under the direction of the master engineer Enrico Martínez. The plan was to construct a tunnel through the mountains at the northwestern corner of the Valley, near Huehuetoca, and to direct the excess water into it by a series of canals. The main canal was designed to drain Lake Zumpango as well as to carry water from the Río de Cuauhtitlan, the largest river of the Valley.

After prodigious labor by thousands of Indians during eleven months in 1607 and 1608, the subterranean channel and its approaches were completed. The mouth of the tunnel was about thirteen feet across and thirteen feet in height, and the whole tunnel was about four miles long. It was excavated in sections, with underground cuts made from a series of perpendicular shafts along its route. At its deepest part it fell approximately 175 feet beneath ground level. The cutting of shafts and the processes of earth removal closely resembled the operations of mine construction. On its far side the tunnel opened at the Boca de San Gregorio, from which waters were conducted by an open trench for a distance of about five miles to empty into the Río de Tula.

In late 1608 the new Desagüe seemed to be complete and successful, requiring only modest improvements and ordinary maintenance. But circumstances quickly rendered it ineffective. The drainage trench from Lake Zumpango became blocked, and the tunnel received water only from the diverted Río de Cuauhtitlan. Martínez's project received criticism as a "negative" Desagüe, one that limited the increase of water levels but did nothing directly to reduce them. In any case, the tunnel was deep enough to drain only Lakes Zumpango and Xaltocan. It could not drain Lake Texcoco, the surface of which was lower than the tunnel's mouth. The tunnel was also criticized for being too small, with an opening too narrow to carry the volume of water that an emergency would require. Even those who criticized it on this score were sometimes unaware that it narrowed deceptively in the interior and that at its narrowest point it measured only about a yard in width and a yard in height. In addition it was imperfectly constructed. Much of its wall consisted of loose earth. Intermittent arches of wood or masonry were insufficient to support its walls and roof, and undermining, crumbling, and blockage occurred. Many new plans were proposed after 1607, including proposals to strengthen the tunnel, to enlarge it, to clear it of obstructions, and to remove its earth cover entirely and convert it to a large open ditch.

When the Spanish court sent the Dutch engineer Adrian Boot to review the Desagüe operations in 1613–14, still another plan was proposed: to abandon the drainage principle entirely and revert to the Indian and sixteenth-century principle of protection by dike. Boot's proposal was for a strong dike, after the manner of Dutch dikes, to separate Lake Texcoco from the waters surrounding the city. The two experts, Enrico Martínez and Adrian Boot, came into conflict over fundamental procedure. New flood waters entered the city in the summer of 1620. Boot asserted in 1622 that everything accomplished so far had been ineffective and that the whole operation had been a waste of money. Viceregal authority, after some vacillation, decided against the tunnel, and work on it was ordered to cease. In 1623, after a brief period of drought, the viceroy ordered the Cuauhtitlan and Tepozotlan rivers redirected into Lake Zumpango in order to test the effectiveness of the tunnel, and the result was a progressive increase in the water level. In 1627 the city's streets were again inundated and large-scale repairs had to be undertaken on these and on the dike. Work on the tunnel began again in 1628, but it was already too late. As the rainy season of 1628 approached, the danger of still more serious flooding in the future was evident to all.

The consequence, in 1629, was the most devastating flood in colonial history. Its immediate cause was the exceptionally heavy rainfall at the opening of the rainy season. Martínez, who had closed the Zumpango channel in order to save the tunnel from the destructive currents, was held responsible for it and placed in jail. The city's canals, which received most of the waste and refuse from the houses, had not been cleaned in the preceding dry season and, with their overflow, the city remained flooded for four years. Streets, plazas, and causeways stood under several feet of water and were again heavily damaged. Canoes and canoeists were brought from surrounding towns for transportation. As the food shortages became acute, three-quarters or more of the city's population fled in a mass evacuation. Houses collapsed. Trade was halted. The king, when informed of the crisis, again proposed the transfer of the city to the mainland.

Reduced rainfall in subsequent years finally brought the great flood to an end. In 1637, with the viceregal transfer of Desagüe control to the Franciscan commissary, Luis Flores, the plan for uncovering the tunnel and converting it into an open trench was implemented. After 1637 most Desagüe labor was applied to the conversion from tunnel to open cut. The tunnel had been constructed, under critical conditions, within a period of eleven months. The transfer to the open cut occupied more than a century. Labor slowed or came completely to a halt during dry periods, only to be vigorously renewed under threat of flood. The transfer to the open cut was finished in the late eighteenth century, but work continued with the object of reducing the pitch of its sides and preventing the sliding of earth into the channel. Thus, with some interruptions and variations in intensity, Desagüe labor was continuous from the early seventeenth century to the end of colonial times.

At all stages of these operations Desagüe labor was regarded as exceptionally arduous. That involving excavation resembled mine labor not only in its character but also in its severity. The repair of causeways required the carrying of stone and earth in large quantities, often in accelerated campaigns of great urgency. Indians were tied to beams at the water's edge and obliged to perform dredging operations while suspended in the current. Darkness, dampness, and cold made the tunnel labor extremely disagreeable. Disease took a heavy toll. Even in the very late colonial period the Indian population was reported to be living in dread of the Desagüe. . . .

The sequestration of Indians for private labor outside encomienda and repartimiento began not on the Spanish farms but in workshops for the production of woolen cloth, known to colonial peoples as obrajes. Although the weaving of cotton was a familiar Indian technique, nothing like the obrajes had been known before the conquest. They were a purely Spanish innovation, a natural corollary of the colonial sheepherding industry, which had established itself very rapidly in central Mexico in the post-conquest years. Woolen looms worked by Indians under Spanish direction were first established in Texcoco in the 1530's or before. During the mid-century period, sheepherding and woolen manufacture enjoyed promotion under the highest auspices. The entrepreneurs included the oidor Lorenzo de Tejada and Antonio de Mendoza, the first viceroy. The obraje thus emerged as a form of labor utilization open to influential non-encomenderos, a fact that may go far to explain its role as a forerunner and prototype in the development of systems of private employment.

The usual obraje was a single enterprise housing its own employees. The technology of manufacture was subdivided and specialized, the chief operations being washing, carding, spinning, and weaving. Most employees were Indians. Negroes and mulattoes were often used as guards. In the early seventeenth century Mexico City had twenty-five obrajes manufacturing cloth and ten manufacturing hats. Texcoco had eight obrajes, Xochimilco four, Azcapotzalco two. They averaged approximately forty-five employees; the smallest required a labor staff of about thirty, while the largest on record in the early seventeenth century had 120 workers.

From the beginning, obraje labor had a sordid reputation. The work was hard, food and living conditions were unsatisfactory, and physical abuse was a commonplace. The mayordomos of obrajes, who were themselves paid in accordance with the obrajes' output, coerced workers with severity and in overtime periods. A captured English sailor, Job Hortop, who was sent to one of the Texcoco obrajes about 1570, spent his time carding wool, as he later reported, "among the Indian slaves." Hortop's companion, Miles Philips, who was similarly sentenced, described his experiences as follows: "We were appointed by the Vice Roy to be carried unto the town of Texcucu . . . in which towne there are certaine houses of correction and punishment for ill people called Obraches, like to Bridwell here in London: into which place divers Indians are sold for slaves, some for ten yeers, and some for twelve." These statements do not represent any English misunderstanding of the status of the obraje workers. Spaniards described the workers in much the same terms, and viceregal laws and other Spanish statements identified them as slaves. Some were Chichimec Indians enslaved during frontier hostilities. More common, however, and historically more interesting for their role in the history of labor procurement, were the Indians condemned for crime, whom Spaniards also regarded as slaves.

In the sentencing of culprits, judges specified terms of service, and obraje operators utilized the convicted workers as private employees. If the sentence took the form of a fine, this might be paid by the employer, who thus "bought" the convict in the same transaction that reimbursed the court. The employer would in turn be reimbursed in labor. The sentences were regarded as differing only in degree from sentences to service in the Philippines or to galley labor in Spain. They were imposed for less serious crimes, and they met an obvious local need. Technically, only members of the audiencia and certain other judges were entitled to issue such sentences. But this technicality was repeatedly disregarded. It came to be the custom that corregidores and their assistants, and other judges, even including Indian gobernadores and the clergy, condemned Indians in the same manner. Viceregal legislation on court jurisdiction makes it clear that judges regularly exceeded their authority in this matter and that they continued to do so to the eighteenth century, often in complicity with the obraje owners.

For the employers, advantages of economy and security lay in possessing a working force of condemned criminals, and judicial sentence provided them with a means of labor procurement far cheaper than Negro slavery. A Negro slave sold for about 400 pesos in the early seventeenth century, and an obraje of average size at this time would thus have required an outlay of some 15,000 to 20,000 pesos for the labor force alone. The obraje employers' self-interest is made emphatic in the protests of the early seventeenth century against royal legislation requiring Negro workers. Convict labor guaranteed to the employer a supply of workers at reduced expense and it allowed time for specialized training. But even in the sixteenth century the obrajes were unable to rely upon criminals alone. Even the widespread abuses in the system of judiciary sentencing were insufficient to satisfy their needs. Moreover, unlike the labradores, the obraje owners could not depend upon repartimiento. Not only were the obraje tasks unsuited to the rotational labor of repartimiento, but repartimiento was commonly held to be inapplicable to obraje conditions on grounds of public good. When obrajes did occasionally receive Indians in repartimiento, this was for peripheral and unskilled tasks, such as the cutting of firewood. In addition, Indian laborers in the obrajes were sometimes regarded as liable to repartimiento drafts in other enterprises, precisely as were the Indians in the towns. It is not surprising, therefore, that the obraje entrepre-

neurs became the first class of employers to develop supplementary techniques of employment, distinct from encomienda, repartimiento, judicial sentence, and Negro slavery.

They began by negotiating privately with individual Indians. It was not difficult to locate native peoples in need of money, and the many stresses of the sixteenth and seventeenth centuries made Indians the more willing to accept offers of employment. The terms of labor were recorded in written contracts, partly because this seemed to fit the royal ideal of voluntary labor. In a contractual agreement the employer and the Indian laborer appeared as free agents, the legal formalities were complied with before royal judges, and the wages, hours, and perquisites of the workers were explicitly set forth. In a colony of corruptible judges, however, contracts were susceptible to many varieties of abuse, all favoring the employers. Judges permitted exploitative contracts and agreed to conditions that would apply in jurisdictions other than their own. Most important, no procedure was ever devised to ensure that the contracts would be fulfilled.

A related technique of the early period was the incarceration of the contracted workers behind locked doors, to make of the obraje, in effect, a prison workshop. Incarceration was already an established procedure by the 1560's, and it may have represented at first only an employer's precaution with respect to a working staff of convicts. But it quickly affected non-convict laborers as well. Viceroy Velasco asserted in his own defense in the 1560's that he had ensured the opening of the obrajes and the removal of guards for the non-criminal employees. We do not know exactly what Velasco accomplished, but it was at best no more than a temporary reform. When the Indian draftsman of Códice Osuna pictured an obraje in Mexico City in the 1560's he carefully delineated its stone façade and massive closed doors. Incarceration continued despite criticism by the church and repeated viceregal denunciation in the late

sixteenth century. It was particularly difficult to control because convicts and other
laborers worked side by side. Royal law
shifted its position and the viceregal administrations legislated rules with distinctions too subtle to be enforced — that
escaped convict workers, for example, might
be compelled "con prisiones" to return to
their labors, while the obrajes themselves
had to be kept open. The law called for a
degree of responsibility that obraje employers refused to assume, and judges continued
to support the employers in defiance of the
law. The obrajes of the seventeenth century contained Indians who had been lured
inside as children under the guise of ap-
prenticeship or committed to obrajes by the
judges as orphans. Once inside, they spent
the remainder of their lives behind locked
or guarded doors. The sentencing of Indians to labor in this manner was still being
forbidden in the eighteenth century. But
the closed obraje persisted until the end of
colonial times.

The sequestration of Indians for private
labor in agriculture has a somewhat different history, much more closely related to
repartimiento. Slave labor and criminal
labor were negligible in agriculture, and
force and incarceration less prevalent. In
agriculture, with the decline of encomienda, repartimiento operated temporarily to
fill the need for labor. Agricultural work
was well adapted to repartimiento; it was
relatively unskilled and was always regarded as falling within the public interest;
it could be adjusted to seasonal demands;
and excess laborers could be channeled into
other employment. It required, however,
an Indian population sufficiently large to
accommodate its uneconomical features.
Probably the epidemic of 1576–81 provided the chief sixteenth-century impetus
to private employment in agriculture, just
as the epidemic of 1545–48 had provided
the chief impetus to repartimiento. Thus
the sequence of agricultural labor institutions — encomienda, repartimiento, private
employment — may be understood as a progressive adjustment to a shrinking labor

supply. As towns failed to supply their repartimiento quotas, labradores undertook to
secure laborers by independent means. Like
obraje owners, labradores made individual
contracts that bound Indian workers to private service. The process was delayed by
the perpetuation of repartimiento, and it
could not succeed completely until repartimiento had been demonstrated to be a
failure. The fifty-year period 1580–1630,
the period of competition between the systems of private and repartimiento labor, was
the critical one in the transformation of
agricultural employment. With every failure of repartimiento, private labor in agriculture gained an additional advantage.
And it was abetted by the circumstance that
private labor in the obrajes had gone before it and established its precedents.

In the wheat farms of the Valley, private
Indian workers (called gañanes) were already being employed by the 1580's. In
1583 the owner of an hacienda near Tepozotlan testified that he had employed
gañanes from Teoloyuca, Tepozotlan, Huehuetoca, and Coyotepec for "many years,"
and he protested against the principales of
the town who were sending his gañanes to
Mexico City as carriers. His complaint was
a typical one, for as labor supplies were
reduced the first impulse of labradores was
to circumvent the gañanes' obligations in
Indian society. In this they received some
viceregal support. The viceroy in 1586
ruled that gañanes were not liable to extra
community tasks. Their sole obligation was
to the repartimiento, and the Indian town
held no other labor claim upon them. With
this rule a labrador might hold his gañanes
at all times of the year except when they
were called to the repartimiento, and the
Spanish institution gained an advantage
over the Indian institution. In test cases —
as in 1599 when the gobernador and alcaldes of Toltitlan sought to use the gañanes
of a labrador in working the fields of Indian
principales — the viceroy took the Spaniard's side and ordered the town authorities
to desist. On occasion Spanish agriculturists influenced the viceroy to rule that

towns could not elect gañanes to local offices. The rule was made explicit with regard to the Indian government of Tlalnepantla in 1604, on the appeal of a local Spaniard.

By the late sixteenth and early seventeenth centuries, then, the agricultural employers were making large strides in the direction of full gañán labor. The principal obstacle at this time was repartimiento itself. Employers continued to receive Indians in repartimiento, but their own gañanes were likewise liable to repartimiento drafts and had to serve other employers when their turns came. Occasionally in the late sixteenth and early seventeenth centuries labradores were permitted to receive their own gañanes in repartimiento drafts, although Indian towns made efforts to prevent this and to use gañanes in other service obligations. Spaniards were likewise sometimes able to receive Indians in repartimiento directly, without attendance at the repartimiento center. Moreover, as repartimiento began to fail conspicuously in the early seventeenth century, those Spaniards possessing gañanes actively encouraged its decline. Their interests now sharply diverged from the interests of those who still had to depend on repartimiento. The employers of gañanes opposed the efforts of jueces repartidores to enlarge or maintain the quotas because—as an interested employer group declared in 1617—any extension of repartimiento would result in the depopulation of the haciendas.

A major period of trial immediately preceded the repartimiento abolition of 1632–33. In the Valley this was a time of epidemic, severe flooding, and the collapse of agricultural repartimiento, virtually all the resources of which were being diverted to the repair of flood damage and to the Desagüe. The Spaniards with gañanes were able to survive, while those who still depended on repartimiento abandoned their farms or shifted, if they could, entirely to gañán labor. Gañanes who had been acquired without legal formality came to occupy positions equivalent to those under

legitimate contract. The crises of the 1620's and early 1630's were radically selective forces in the transformation of agricultural employment. In repartimiento jurisdictions such as Tacuba-Azcapotzalco, where the number of operating wheat farms fell from two hundred to sixty, the abolition order of 1632–33 could appear only as a coup-de-grâce. In 1601, when the monarchy had sought to abolish repartimiento, the labradores had not been ready for abolition and had successfully opposed it. But by 1633 it could not affect them; repartimiento was an institution they had already rejected and passed beyond.

Within Indian society, the 1620's brought about another kind of selectivity. Here the division lay between those Indians responsible for the maintenance of community obligations and those who found a personal solution in becoming gañanes. The crises of these years served as inducements to Indians to seek employment in haciendas, and in some instances to move completely from town to hacienda residence. To Indian refugees from the towns the hacienda offered an escape, and the interests of the hacendados and the gañanes converged in opposition to traditional community obligation. The situation contributed to a conflict between Indian communities and Spanish haciendas, a conflict that continued into the twentieth century. But in the early seventeenth century the lines of division were still far from clear. Many gañanes were residents of towns. In Texcoco, where the normal tendencies favoring gañán labor operated side by side with a developed obraje economy in 1630, three-quarters of the Indian population were in direct non-repartimiento service to Spaniards. In Tequixquiac, where the surviving encomendero was an influential hacendado, the Indian gobernador took the hacendado's side and compelled Indians to labor in the hacienda. Caciques and other Indians who themselves became hacendados opposed the Indian town officers who sought to divert the hacienda workers to community tasks. The hacienda was the culminating institution in the long history of Indian agricultural labor, but it was less overtly coercive in its policies of labor recruitment than any of the antecedent institutions. Enslavement, encomienda, repartimiento, and the obrajes all required compulsion. The hacienda did not, at least to the same degree. The hacienda was not a simple institution. Its internal operation and its relation to the economic environment were intricate and shifting. Its role was one of progressive domination over land, over agriculture, and over other forms of supply, and as it dominated these it necessarily extended its control over Indian labor. The hacienda could afford to reject outright coercion in the procurement of workers because the accumulation of other pressures upon Indian society had rendered such coercion unnecessary. Haciendas had no need of the prison atmosphere of the obrajes. The economic environment had developed, or deteriorated, to the point at which the hacienda, for all its rigors, offered positive advantages to Indian workers.

These observations would appear to conflict with the common assumption that the hacienda acquired and retained its workers through debt servitude. It has been argued, quite plausibly, that hacendados, like other employers of Indian labor, did use coercion, that they contrived to become the creditors of individual Indians and thereafter compelled debtors to labor in discharge of the amount owed. An examination of this thesis in relation to labor in the Valley will require first a survey of the history of wages and other remunerations in the types of labor thus far discussed.

Most early labor — in encomienda, in urban construction, or in other duties — was either unrecompensed or recompensed only with respect to the Indian officers responsible for the delivery of workers. Labor hired for wages, however, is recorded occasionally for both skilled and unskilled workmen in the 1530's and after. As of 1549, before the separation of the agricultural repartimiento from labor in the city, the nor-mal wage for a day's hire in unskilled labor was one cuartillo (one-fourth real, or 8½ maravedís) per day. This was officially rejected as inadequate recompense, and under Viceroy Velasco's rule in the early 1560's wages were set at $^6/_{17}$ real (12 maravedís) per day for unskilled workers (*peones*) in the labor drafts on the farms and $^{12}/_{17}$ real (24 maravedís) for carpenters, masons, and other skilled workers (*oficiales*) laboring principally at urban tasks. In the repartimiento for farms all workers were regarded as unskilled. Wages were increased to one-half and one real per day respectively in 1553, and hence Indian laborers were receiving one-half real per day in 1555, when the agricultural repartimiento was formally separated as a distinct institution. The wage was increased to two-thirds and then to three-fourths real for peones in the 1560's and 1570's, and to one real for unskilled and two reales for skilled workers in several enactments around 1590. Wages for peones in repartimiento were raised to 1½ reales per day in the period 1603–10 and to two reales per day by 1629.

Wages for unskilled hired labor outside repartimiento approximated the repartimiento figures but were more variable. In the 1560's wages for unskilled hired labor varied from one-fourth real per day in Xochimilco to 1½ reales per day in Mexico City. Skilled craftsmen working outside repartimiento were earning at this time one-half real per day in Xochimilco and 3 to 4 reales in Mexico City. Skilled workers practicing their own trades in Mexico City in the late sixteenth and early seventeenth centuries received up to 8 reales (one peso) per day. Hired agricultural labor by peones was recompensed at a normal rate of 1½ reales per day in the early seventeenth century. Labor services for corregidores were to be paid for at a rate of one real per day in the 1590's. In obrajes a wage of 3 to 4 pesos per month, amounting to one real per day or less, was common in the early seventeenth century. The cost of hiring substitutes in repartimiento labor ranged up to double the repartimiento pay, rising from 8 reales per week in 1570 to 10 or 12 reales in the 1590's, and to 18 reales per week in the 1620's. In the late sixteenth century a skilled Indian worker might avoid his week's repartimiento obligation through a payment to the employer of 3 or 4 pesos (4 to 5 reales per day). In obligatory service to Indian gobernadores and caciques, peones of the sixteenth century received much more modest sums, generally 20 or 25 cacaos and daily food.

Desagüe labor was paid for by the state — unlike agricultural labor which was paid for by the private employers — and it accordingly received a lower wage. Few if any of the albarradón workers of 1555–56 received compensation. The Desagüe plans of 1604–5 called for a wage of one peso per week, but the first workers of the seventeenth century received nothing. Later the Desagüe wage rose from 5 to 7 reales per week in 1620, to 9 reales by 1628, and to 12 reales per week or two reales per day by the 1640's.

Wages for Indian labor in each category thus increased during the period of population decline. From the 1630's to the end of the colonial period, on the other hand, wages were much more stable. Rates in the late eighteenth century were in some cases identical with those of a hundred and fifty years before. "Free" workers in late colonial obrajes still received only 3 pesos per month. The common daily wages for peones at the time of the abolition of agricultural repartimiento — 1½ or 2 reales per day — remained standard until the last quarter of the eighteenth century. The hacienda wage was commonly 2 reales per working day for peones, with equivalent rates for other employees: 2 reales per day for mule keepers and field workers; 1½ or 2 reales per day for cowherds and their helpers; one real per day for shepherds, youths, and miscellaneous assistants; and 3 or 4 reales per day for skilled masons. At the end of the eighteenth century wages for peones varied between 1½ and 2½, and

oficiales were commanding wages of 3 to 5 reales per day. The highest recorded peones' wage is 3 reales per day in the early nineteenth century.

To these wage scales were added, under certain circumstances, provision of daily food and extra pay for travel to or from work. In repartimiento and Desagüe labor, five or six leagues (approximately fifteen miles) of travel were regarded as the equivalent of one day of labor, and, with a variety of exceptions, were paid for accordingly. Travel did not normally figure in the wages paid by haciendas. The provision of food to workers was common in obrajes and in the late repartimientos, including the Desagüe. Food provision in haciendas was standard and universal, but the provisions were not always in addition to the wage. If the wage were two reales per day, one might be issued in money and the other as a maize ration; alternatively, the full monetary payment might be made and a part received back by the hacienda in maize sales. Even haciendas that did not produce maize for sale customarily raised a supply for their own workers. Haciendas commonly issued monetary wages on Sunday — this ensured that workers would have the means to meet their ecclesiastical obligations — and deferred the maize payments to Tuesday or Wednesday, after the weekly labor had begun. As the manager of the hacienda of Molino de Flores, near Texcoco, stated in 1785, this schedule was deliberately established and had "a thousand advantages," for it meant that the workers would be induced to stay on the premises.

Debt labor, like much else in labor history, received its earliest impetus in the obrajes and spread from them to other employment institutions. Debt could be incurred in many ways. An advance in wages to a "free" obraje laborer placed him immediately in debt. An Indian laborer might be forced to accept money payable in work, or he might be required to purchase, with borrowed funds, the equipment he was to use in obraje labor. Deductions might be made against a worker's account if his finished cloth weighed less than the raw wool with which he started. Forced sales, with price markups and the prohibition of purchases elsewhere, might prolong or increase his debt.

Royal legislation on debt labor in the sixteenth century sometimes forbade loans by employers to their workers and the discharge of debt by labor. But other rules tended to compromise in favor of the employers. As in so many other matters, laws shifted between prohibition and regulation. Loans were to be transacted before judges, but other loans, for tribute or for food or for "necessities," could be transacted privately. Restrictions were placed upon the amount of loans and on the periods for which debts could be effective. Viceregal legislation in 1595 supported the employers even to the point of forbidding payments of debt in money and specifying payments in labor. But labor debts were entirely forbidden again by royal and viceregal legislation in the early seventeenth century. When communities had to perform special Desagüe labor in commutation of tribute arrears, a supervised public debt servitude was established. Limitations on the duration of the debts were attempted, as well as limitations on the amounts, expressed as salary for a given number of months. The law also recognized those employers who paid tributes for their Indian employees, tribute payment sometimes being regarded as a separate transaction, not to be included in computing the maximum legal debt.

No one could argue that the Valley's hacendados absolutely refrained from using the devices of debt employment, for countless records indicate that they did use them. But many other employers used them as well, and one must be cautious in evaluating the special role of debt employment in haciendas. A comparison between the hacienda and the obraje is revealing here, for while both were institutions of debt labor, the obraje was in addition a closed and guarded workshop. Obraje history indicates that debt labor alone was incapable of hold-

ing obraje workers, and it may be concluded that it was likewise incapable of holding hacienda workers. In any case, indebtedness was a legal technicality. An Indian worker bent on leaving his hacienda could find occasion to do so despite his indebtedness — just as any Indian could default and escape his tribute debt to a town or his private debt to any creditor. From the viceregal point of view, even the legal technicality could be regarded as inapplicable in the late eighteenth century, for the viceroy was on record in 1784 with the assertion that Indians might freely leave the haciendas regardless of the amount they owed.

An examination of hacienda records is further revealing. During any agricultural year the working force of a large Valley hacienda might vary from fifty to three hundred or more persons, depending on the seasonal demand for agricultural labor. The nucleus of this labor force consisted of resident workers, the "gañanes radicados" of the hacienda, who might be expected to work regularly six days a week. For the remainder of their workers haciendas relied on a fluid supply from nearby communities. The seasonal operations entailed a continuous influx and departure of workers, under conditions quite different from those of the closed obraje. . . .

Present evidence for the Valley suggests that in late colonial times debt peonage affected fewer than half the workers on haciendas, and that the large majority of these owed debts equal to three weeks' labor or less. But a full explanation for the hold of the hacienda over its workers cannot stop with debt servitude. To Indian workers the hacienda offered solutions to economic conditions not to be found elsewhere. As monetary values came to occupy a large role in Indian society — in tribute, in ecclesiastical charges, in economic exchange — the hacienda offered a regular or irregular income. To Indians who had lost their lands (largely, of course, to haciendas) the hacienda provided a dwelling and a means of livelihood. Under conditions permitting only tiny margins between income and sustenance, the hacienda was an institution of credit, allowing Indians freely to fall behind in their financial obligations without losing their jobs or incurring punishment.

If these conclusions are accurate, we confront the further problem of explaining the evil reputation of the hacienda in Mexican labor history. In part, this reputation may represent an extension, with respect to labor, of a reputation gained in acts of land usurpation. In part, it may relate to areas remote from the Valley or to areas where haciendas were larger and workers less numerous. It may also reflect conditions of the nineteenth century and attitudes of justification relating to the Revolution of 1910, for in the national period Indian enslavement and repartimiento were obsolescent, and industrialization depended upon a mestizo urban population. In rural areas, where Indian civilization persisted, only the hacienda exploited labor, and an Indianist ideology consequently focused its attention here. But in the Valley in colonial times the hacienda offered an acceptable livelihood to Indians who had lost their lands. The alternatives—starvation, vagabondage, abandonment of town and family—were less attractive for most workers than hacienda labor itself. Moreover, the same hacienda labor might appear moderate in comparison with other circumstances of the colonial period, and harsh only in comparison with a twentieth-century liberal ideal. To say this is to suggest that in areas such as the Valley of Mexico Indian labor for Spanish employers became progressively less severe, and that it became least severe under the hacienda.

SUGGESTIONS FOR ADDITIONAL READING

The selections chosen for inclusion in this volume can serve as an introduction to the subject of Spanish-Indian relations, but they are an introduction. In the event that a student may wish to pursue the subject more intensively the following authors and works are listed. For some readers the lack of a reading command of Spanish will make many of these bibliographical notes rather useless. An attempt is made to note pertinent works in English; but at the outset the unilingual reader is forewarned to be prepared for disappointment.

Only one major study by Lesley Byrd Simpson *The Encomienda in New Spain* (1950 ed.), has been noted, even though his edition of the Laws of Burgos has been borrowed and his Research Lecture has been reprinted. The student might like to compare this revised edition of *The Encomienda* with the original by the same name published in 1929. Mention should be made of his *Many Mexicos* (New York, 1946, and Berkeley and Los Angeles, 1952), which has much on the present topic. Attention should also be called to four shorter studies, which appeared as Nos. 7, 13, and 16 of the Ibero-Americana Series: *Studies in the Administration of the Indians in New Spain* (Berkeley and Los Angeles, 1934–40).

The student is encouraged to read the whole of the work by Lewis Hanke from which the selection in this volume was taken, *The Spanish Struggle for Justice in the Conquest of America* (Philadelphia, 1949). This study, awarded the Beveridge Prize by the American Historical Association in 1947, touches many aspects of conquistador-Indian relations. Hanke's interest in this topic was first evidenced in *The First Social Experiments in America* (Cambridge, 1935). The interest led him, quite naturally, into the controversy in which Las Casas was one of the main figures and has turned him into the foremost interpre-ter, in English at least, of the life and work of the bellicose friar. Among his many writings on Las Casas and cognate subjects are *Bartolomé de Las Casas, An Interpretation of His Life and Writings* (The Hague, 1951); *Bartolomé de Las Casas, Bookman, Scholar and Propagandist* (Philadelphia, 1952); *Aristotle and the American Indians* (Chicago, 1959). He has authored numerous articles which have appeared in journals in the several Americas and abroad.

Robert S. Chamberlain, besides the study included here on the labor practices of the Mayas, also investigated another prediscovery field with his *Castilian Backgrounds of the Repartimiento-Encomienda* (Washington, 1939).

Attention should be called to excellent chapters on the Indians and their relation to the Spaniards in Clarence H. Haring, *The Spanish Empire in America* (New York, 1947). Chapter III, particularly, offers a fine overview of the labor problem and its developing solutions.

Of the Latin American historians Silvio Zavala of Mexico has been the most productive student of the subject under consideration. In the same little volume from which the chapter included in this collection was taken, *New Viewpoints on the Spanish Colonization of America,* there are several more which touch the topic of Indian labor. His *La encomienda indiana* (Madrid, 1935) is one of the classics in the field; he had preceded this with *Los intereses particulares en la conquista de la Nueva España* (Madrid, 1933), which at least brushes our topic. Several later studies are much more germane: *De encomiendas y propiedad territorial en algunas regiones de la América española* (Mexico, 1940); *Servidumbre natural y libertad cristiana, según los tratadistas españoles de los siglos XVI y XVII* (Buenos Aires, 1944); *Contribución a la historia de las instituciones coloniales en Guatemala* (Mexico, 1945). With

María Castelo he edited eight volumes, *Fuentes para la historia del trabajo en Nueva España* (Mexico, 1939–46).

Several Latins have done studies on specific areas of the Latin Americas: Domingo Amunátegui Solar, *Las encomiendas indíjenas de Chile* (3 vols.; Santiago 1909–10); Manuel Belaunde Guinassi, *La encomienda en Perú* (Lima, 1945); Vicente Dávila, *Encomiendas* (3 vols.; Caracas, 1925–45); Moises González Navarro, *Repartimiento de indias en Nueva Galicia* (Mexico, 1953); Enrique de Gandía, *Francisco de Alfaro y la condición social de los indios, Río de la Plata, Paraguay, y Tucumán y Perú, siglos XVI y XVII* (Buenos Aires, 1939); Guillermo Feliú Cruz y Carlos Monge Alfaro, *Las encomiendas según tasas y ordenanzas* (Buenos Aires, 1941).

The Mexican historian José Miranda studies a vital aspect of the Indian problem in his *El tributo indigena en la Nueva España en el siglo XVI* (Mexico, 1952); there are other pertinent views in *Vitoria y los intereses de la conquista de América* (Mexico, 1947). The same may be said of Charles Gibson, *The Aztecs under Spanish Rule* (Stanford, 1964), from which one chapter has been taken for this volume. José María Arboleda Llorente, *El indio en la colonia* (Bogotá, 1948) will well repay perusal. So, too, José Maria Ots Capdequí, *Instituciones sociales de la América española en el período colonial* (La Plata, 1934).

Zavala touches on the question of Indian slavery, as do several of the other authors already cited. One of the longer treatments of the subject is that of José A. Saco, *Historia de la esclavitud de los indios del Nuevo Mundo* (2 vols., Habana, 1932).

Something has previously been said of the seventeenth century Spanish jurist León Pinelo. The *Política indiana* (1648) of Juan de Solórzano Pereira gives another jurist's view of the *encomienda, servicio personal,* and other related problems growing out of Spain's empire overseas. In general, he defends the Crown and the Spaniards. Several other writers of the colonial centuries should be noted. Juan de Mati-

enzo, *oidor* of the Audiencia de Charcas, wrote a treatise entitled *Gobierno del Perú,* probably in the 1570's — the first two books were published in Buenos Aires, 1910. Pedro de Aguado's *Historia de Santa Marta y Nuevo Reino de Granada* was written in the third quarter of the sixteenth century and edited for publication in 1916. There have been several editions of José de Acosta, *Historia natural y moral de las Indias.* Enlightening is the sixteenth-century work of the Franciscan, Fray Toribio de Benavente Motolinía, *Historia de los indios de la Nueva España* (late edition, Mexico, 1941); the selection in this volume has called attention to the English translation by Steck. The work of Alonso de Zorita, *Historia de la Nueva España,* to give it a very abbreviated title, has been published in at least two twentieth-century editions. Obviously, no one should try to go deeply into this Indian problem without reading widely from the many works of Bartolomé de Las Casas — *Historia de las Indias, Apologética historia de las Indias, Brevísima relación de la destrucción de las Indias,* to mention only some of the principal writings of the indefatigable "Protector of the Indians."

Two older English writers have views on the Spanish treatment of the Indians: William Robertson, *History of America* (2 vols.; London, 1777), and Sir Arthur Helps, *The Spanish Conquest in America and Its Relation to the History of Slavery and to the Government of the Colonies* (4 vols.; London, 1885–61; new edition by M. Oppenheimer, 1900–1904). Some rather damning Spanish views can be found in José María Chacón y Calvo, *Cartas censorías de la conquista* (Habana, 1938), and in Genaro García, *Carácter de la conquista española en América y en México, según textos de los historiadores primitivos* (Mexico, 1901).

The Laws of Burgos have been reproduced in this volume. There is a recent edition by Antonio Muro Orejón of the New Laws, *Las leyes nuevas, 1542–1543* (Sevilla, 1946), with the documents from the Archivo de Indias and the modern transcription; *The New Laws of the Indies,* ed. Henry Stevens (London, 1893), gives a translation. Mention has been made earlier in this volume of the great code of the Indies, *Recopilación de leyes de los reynos de las Indias,* first published in 1681 and revised in 1756, both editions in four volumes.

This listing has not tried to record the many shorter studies which have appeared in various historical journals in the last several decades, for reasons of length. The interested reader is referred to the bibliographies in the books of Hanke, Simpson, Gibson, and Zavala, for such helps to further study. As Hanke remarks, this is still a field of colonial Latin American history whose surface has been barely scratched and which can offer the researcher rich rewards and much satisfaction.